Crochet Mastery

[7 Books in 1] - Your Ultimate Crash Course From Novice to Expert, with Step-by-Step DIY Projects to Master the Art of Crocheting. Including Amigurumi Patterns.

By

Lana Dillard

Crochet in the rounds, row, chain and pattern. 30

   CROCHET IN THE ROUND, ROWS AND MORE. 30

      Counting Crochet Stitches 32

      How To Count Crochet Rounds/Rows 33

   CHAIN STITCH IN CROCHET 34

      Chain Stitch Tips 35

   SLIP STITCH 36

      Joining a Crochet Round or Making a Ring 37

      Slip Stitches in Surface Crochet 38

      More Ways to Use Slip Stitch 38

   SINGLE CROCHET 39

      Tips for Beginners 40

   HALF DOUBLE CROCHET STITCH (HDC) 41

      Tips For Working With Half Double Crochet In Different Manners 45

   DOUBLE CROCHET STITCH 46

   TREBLE CROCHET 52

   MAGIC LOOP. 59

   READING CROCHET PATTERNS. 63

      Basic Stitch Abbreviations 63

Book 3: 70

Crochet mistakes, tricks and secrets 70

   CROCHET TROUBLESHOOTING TIPS 70

      Crochet tips for straight edges 74

Book 4. 80

Crochet Projects for Beginners. 80

   Easy Crochet Patterns for Beginners 80

      Potholder 80

      Easy Crochet Scarf Pattern 84

      Chunky Ribbed Beanie 89

      Crochet Hair Scrunchie 92

      Crochet a Granny Square 94

Book 5. 100

Crochet projects for intermediates 100

Lace Jewels Hooded Scarf Free Crochet Pattern 100

Fluffy Meringue Shawl 102

Mountain Breeze Poncho 102

Moroccan Tile Afghan 103

Mosaic Motifs Blanket 104

Book 6. 106

Crochet projects for advanced 106

Crochet Peppermint Throw 106

Spiderweb Blanket 107

Textured Bavarian Pillow 108

Bean Stitch Bag 109

Sun Blossom Mandala Doily 110

Book 7. 111

Amigurumi crochet projects patterns 111

a Rainbow of Monsters 111

Amigurumi duck 117

Amigurumi Whale Pattern 117

Amigurumi Turtle 118

Amigurumi Cow 119

Conclusion 120

Why you must acquire this skill 120

BONUS 124

INTRODUCTION

A single hook of any size and yarn or thread can be used to manufacture toys, clothing, lace, and fabric through the technique of crocheting. Hats, purses, and jewelry can all be made using crochet.

The name "crochet," as it is known in English, comes from the French word "croche," which means hook. Crochet stitches are created by dragging the yarn through an active loop, just like in knitting. Crocheting simply needs one loop or stitch at a time, but knitting requires a row of open active loops. By altering the tension, adding and removing stitches, and wrapping the yarn around the hook while making a stitch, one may create a multitude of textures, patterns, and shapes.

The variety of materials available for crocheting is endless. People from all across the world have utilized thread, wool, yarn, grass, rope, wire, silk, and even crocheted hair and dental floss throughout history.

Many people believe that Chinese needlework, a very old type of embroidery seen in Turkey, India, Persia, and North Africa, is most likely where crochet originated. It arrived in Europe in the 1700s and was called "tambouring," from the French word "tambour," which means drum. When the background cloth was eliminated and the stitch was created on its own, tambour became what the French referred to as "crochet in the air" around the end of the 18th century.

Exchanging Knowledge of Crochet

For a very long time, friends and relatives would verbally teach each other how to crochet; patterns and stitches were taken straight from the source material. The more times an item was replicated, the more inaccurately it was made and the more it deviated from the original design.

The basic notion that particular stitches could be learned and communicated via a tiny sample that could be manufactured and maintained as the primary reference in each home developed from this practice. Eventually, stitch samples were created and sewn onto leftover paper to create a kind of soft book that was circulated throughout women's groups.

BOOK 1:
CROCHET 101, HISTORY AND MAIN TECHNIQUES

We immediately picture grandmothers when we hear the word "crochet." Our brains haven't naturally trained to link to one another for such a long time. Nevertheless, crocheting isn't only a pastime for our grandmothers anymore. If not, more adults and young people than ever before are practicing it.

Crochet is a needlework technique that is done using a crochet hook and yarn or another material that is similar, according to its global definition. Typically, the substance in question is yarn or thread. Alternative materials that can be used include fabric, wire, twine, or any creative material.

CROCHET'S OBJECTIVE.

If it isn't obvious now, the primary purpose of crocheting is for us, the practitioners – the crochet fans — to finish particular items. These projects are usually things that are beautiful, practical, or extremely advantageous in one way or another. Baby blankets, baby booties, warm scarves, handbags, shawls, tote bags, afghans, and a ton more are great examples of large-scale crochet crafts. And if you believe that crochet ends there, I implore you to reconsider. You may also make amazing drapes, stockings, and jewelry with crochets.

Furthermore, other components for already produced products can also be crocheted. As a preferred example, consider creative crochet trims and adorable or amazing edgings. Such can be used to crocheted items or previous tasks that you have completed. Knitted products, sewn items, and even items you have previously purchased should be brought to the closest store. What better way to personalize your just acquired socks, towels, or pillowcases than with a gorgeous crocheted border?

While finishing their individual projects is the ultimate goal for the majority of crafters, not all of them are solely focused on that. Crocheting offers advantages, ambitions, and rewards beyond projects alone. A calming and contemplative activity, crocheting can be. It may be quite fulfilling to watch your handmade effort come to life and provide such a fulfilling delight.

KNITTING AND CROCHETING

You might assume that knitting and crocheting are the same after just one glance. People frequently confuse them since they do have many things in common, such as the use of colored yarns for project creation in both practices. It is feasible for afghans, shawls, hats, scarves, sweaters, and other items to develop identically on both methods. One cannot hold it against someone who isn't very knowledgeable about knitting or crocheting if they can't quickly distinguish between the two. Ultimately, the distinctions between the two are becoming increasingly hazy due to a number of techniques that enable practitioners to produce items that were formerly limited to knitting.

But soon, if you examine each closely, you'll notice what appears to be a difference between them. By seeing the tools that an individual is actively using, you may determine if they are knitting or crocheting. If you see someone with a hook, they are crocheting; if you see someone with two pointed needles, or even a circular needle, they are knitting. Then there are artisans who knit and crochet together for a specific purpose. For instance, they attached a crocheted border to a knitted garment. To be honest, the possibilities for these two DIY pastimes seem limitless.

3 OF THE MOST BASIC CROCHET TERMS

The crochet stitch is the most essential term in the crocheting language. Its definition is also as clear as it can be: it is the crochet stitching style. Every crochet project uses a certain type of crochet stitch. The simplest crochet stitches are listed below, which you should be completely familiar with:

The Chain Stitch.

If you want the practice of crocheting to become a part of you, learning chain stitching is essential. The initial stage in a certain crochet craft is often to make a series of interlocking chain stitches, aside from the slip knot. Learning how to chain stitch is the first step in crocheting.

With your hook held up, face up. Loop working yarn over hook from back to front while crochet hook is still inside slip knot. When you hook the thread, rotate your crochet hook counterclockwise by about 1/4 of a turn. Once the yarn is securely hooked, pull it through the slip knot to finish your first chain stitch.

Hook and drag through another loop to begin the next chain stitch. Iterate the procedure as many times as required. You would quickly discover that this is simple and begin to create chain stitches with a lovely rhythm.

Slip Stitch.

Another fundamental crochet stitch that every hobbyist has to master is the slip stitch. The slip stitch is used for finishing items with a basic border, adding ornamental components, and joining sections together.

Almost anytime after you start a project, you can work a slip stitch. Put your hook into the desired crochet slip stitch location if it already has an active loop on it. Next, hook your yarn. Later on in the project, pull the thread up through it.

Lastly, drag the just formed loop across the hook's active loop. That's it, the slip stitch is finished. With a little repetition of the instructions provided, it will nearly become a seamless motion.

Single Crochet Stitch.

To be proficient in the hobby, you need to learn yet another crochet stitch. Single crochet stitches are used in most crochet patterns and applications. But fear not—one of the simplest stitches to learn is the single crochet. You now have an endless number of applications for it once you've mastered it. A single crochet stitch can be used to work rows, in rounds, spirals, as an edging, and much more.

Put the hook through the initial chain. Put your hook into the single crochet stitch in the row just below it for the second row and on. Underneath each of the chain's two loops, slide the hook. Now that the hook is in position, get ready to sketch out a circle. Grasp the yarn with your hook after wrapping it around it.

Make sure the working yarn and hook are pulled through the loops you made. By now, your hook ought to be covered in two stitches. Re-wrap the yarn around your hook, then hook it. Catch the yarn by re-wrapping it around your hook. Pull the hook and insert the thread through the hook's two loops. The single crochet stitch is finished in this phase. Although it might seem complicated at first, once you complete your first single crochet, the others will seem incredibly simple.

These are only a few examples of common terminology used in the crocheting community. If you dive straight in, you will eventually uncover a ton more. However, you must first become proficient in the three previously listed crochet stitches before moving on to the more intricate ones. And once you have, you'll find that the subsequent stitches are already rather simple. Now go off and start working on your first or next project.

HISTORY

What comes to mind when you think of crochet? Maybe the first thing that comes to mind is the adorable little baby booties for the newest member of your family, or the afghan that used to sit on the back of your grandparents' couch when you were a child.

French is where crochet originated.

Crochet is the technique of creating loops and interlocking them together to produce daily products we love, such as a comforting blanket, a gorgeous doily for your buffet, or a fluffy hat to wear in the winter. Crochet is derived from the French word "croche," which means "crochet." Like many other crafts, crocheting was born out of need. A hook and some yarn or thread can be used to make a variety of practical goods for daily use, like blankets, scarves, and washcloths, as well as entertaining items like toys or amigurumi stuffed animals.

derived from the tambour art

It is difficult to say for sure when crochet was first invented, but studies have indicated that it most likely came from tambour, an old Chinese needlework method that used cloth, thread, and a needle with a hook on the end. Stretched taut over a frame, the fabric resembles an embroidery hoop. A sharp hook is used to puncture holes in the fabric. A thread, typically with beads attached, is caught by the hook beneath the fabric and pulled through. This produces incredibly intricate and fine designs all over the cloth.

The original crochet pattern

It is possible that the origins of modern crochet occurred in Europe in the early 1800s, and word about it spread from there. Similar to tambour, although without the taut cloth and frame, a hook is employed here. Mademoiselle Riego de la Branchardiere created the first crochet design that is known to exist in 1824. She transformed already-famous needlework and embroidery motifs into crochet patterns that could be used with a hook and thread. Cotton yarn was made tougher and less prone to break in 1844 when it was treated with sodium hydroxide as part of the mercerization process, which also made cotton yarn more widely available.

As the Great Irish Potato Famine struck in the middle of the 1840s, families turned to crochet to generate the money they sorely needed to survive and to travel abroad in search of a better life. Crochet's popularity only grew from there. Irish families, to mention a few, found eager and willing clients in London, Dublin, and Paris where they wove elaborate lace. Every member of the family would frequently be given a single theme or piece of the lace to make, and at the conclusion, the lace would be crocheted together to incorporate all of the pieces.

Crochet for war troops

Although the exact date of crochet's arrival in America is unknown, it is believed to have existed during the Civil War. In one of her books, Laura Ingalls Wilder (1867–1957) mentioned that she had made her older sister Mary a lace headpiece out of crochet.

In World Wars I and II, the government promoted women to knit and crochet essential things for the troops, like gloves, hats, and warm scarves. This helped crochet become a part of the war effort. Even something as basic as warm socks might have a significant impact on American men in the trenches. Their feet were easily chilly since their boots lacked insulation, especially when they got wet. To keep their feet warm and dry, most soldiers wore two pairs of socks at a time, provided they had any.

The boom of the granny square

The hippie milieu of the 1960s and 1970s gave rise to a boom in the popularity of crocheted objects, particularly the renowned crochet granny square. A granny square is a square that is made by crocheting in rounds, starting in the middle and working outward. During this time, brightly colored yarn was very fashionable, and vests, sweaters, and other clothing frequently had various colors.

Aiming to create miniature, plush animals or characters, amigurumi is a Japanese craft that helped crochet gain popularity in the early 2000s. Amigurumi characters are usually brightly colored, attractive, and have huge eyes that resemble cartoons. They are usually crocheted in the round. Because they are small, amigurumi stuffed animals make excellent gifts and require less time to produce than other crochet crafts.

An increase in the quantity of expert crocheters

Crocheting has evolved from being a necessity to a pastime throughout time. Purchasing the necessary items is not only quicker, but also easier. You don't need to design your own scarf because they come in every hue under the sun. Nonetheless, a sizable portion of the population still works full-time as crocheters, producing and selling their creations. Handmade goods have become more and more popular over the last ten or so years, particularly since the emergence of websites like as Etsy and Amazon Handmade (in 2005 and 2015, respectively). Consumers are preferring longer-lasting products, appreciating quality, and supporting local companies.

The creativity and fun of crocheting are accessible to even the most famous people! Notable celebrities who crochet are Wheel of Fortune's Vanna White, Meryl Streep, and Cher. Vanna actually has a yarn brand of her own, "Vanna's Choice," with Lion Brand. Katy Perry is another well-known star who crochets. In a 2016 interview with Alan Carr, Katy discussed her passion for crocheting and stated that she likes to work on it before going to bed in order to unwind.

THE FUTURE OF CROCHET

The history of crochet has been discussed, but what about its future? I believe that crocheting—as well as creating in general—will continue to gain popularity as more and more people gravitate toward purchasing handcrafted goods. Due to the COVID-19 epidemic last year, hobby making has become extremely popular since more people were forced to stay at home and have more time to pick up new skills. It appears that crochet becomes more popular during difficult or turbulent times, whether due to necessity (as during World Wars I and II) or for amusement (like during the most recent surge during the epidemic).

THE HEALTH BENEFITS OF CROCHET

The American Counseling Association states that the most frequently mentioned and researched advantage of crocheting is its ability to alleviate depression. It has been demonstrated that practicing the skill repeatedly releases serotonin, a natural antidepressant. Furthermore, after crocheting, 81% of respondents with depression reported feeling cheerful, and more than half reported feeling "very happy" in a different study that was published in The British Journal of Occupational Therapy. In general, crafting promotes the development of new talents, which helps to increase self-esteem. It also fosters a sense of productivity, offers a rewarding means of giving to others, and facilitates the creation of beautiful things through expression.

Crocheting has numerous physical health benefits as well. It has been demonstrated that counting stitches is a straightforward and effective way for persons suffering from anxiety related to obsessive compulsive disorder (OCD). The brain has to work hard to perform bilateral, accurate, and coordinated hand movements. We are consequently less able to focus on other problems and issues. This supports the idea of "staying in the moment," which is a suggested mindfulness exercise.

Mindfullness.

The NHS defines mindfulness as an awareness of oneself and the environment. Moreover, it can benefit our mental health. It is commonly established that rhythmic, repetitive motion can help us relax when we are under stress. Anxiety crutches like pacing, rocking, tapping, and hair pulling are common. Crocheting in their place has shown to be a huge assistance. The lack of eye contact required when crocheting in a group is an additional intriguing physical benefit. Self-conscious, shy, anxious, and socially uncomfortable people typically handle situations better when it is completely permissible for them to make eye contact only when they wish. Though, when it comes to greetings, general politeness is encouraged. Given this, having a discussion isn't essential in a crocheting group. This gives them back some control by creating a "feeling-safe" environment in which they can decide whether or not to communicate.

ESSENTIAL CROCHET TOOLS

Are you unsure of the supplies required to begin crocheting? If so, you're at the proper location. This post is a comprehensive list of the necessary crocheting supplies and tools that every beginner needs.

For a list of the essential crocheting supplies you really need to get started, keep reading.

Having the proper supplies is essential while learning how to crochet. You will learn much more quickly and enjoyably if you have the high-quality tools and creative supplies you require.

However, it might be challenging to determine which supplies are truly necessary and which ones can wait until later if you're just starting out with crocheting.

We'll outline the most important crochet supplies and tools you'll need as a beginner in this chapter.

We'll start by discussing the basic things you'll need to get going. These will be referred to as "need to haves."

Next, we'll discuss some additional crochet supplies that you might wish to purchase to make crocheting more enjoyable and easier. We'll refer to those as the "nice to haves." To get you started on the right path, we'll also provide you some advice on selecting the appropriate yarn and hooks for your projects.

So, continue reading for a list of my top beginner crochet equipment, regardless of your level of competence or desire to expand your stash!

BEST CROCHET SUPPLIES FOR BEGINNERS

The crochet hook and yarn are the two most essential crocheting instruments, as one might expect. You won't be able to crochet anything without these two items!

To complete your crochet toolkit, you'll also need a yarn needle, scissors, stitch markers, and a measuring tape in addition to the hook and yarn.

The favorable tidings? You can easily find all of these supplies online or at your neighborhood craft stores.

Let's take a closer look at each of these crocheting supplies and tools.

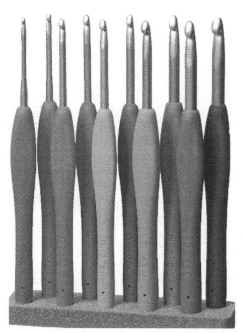

Crochet Hooks

Let's start by discussing the most important tool of all: the crochet hook.

In contrast to knitting, which calls for two needles, crochet just needs one hook.

There are plenty of alternatives available to you when looking for the best crochet hooks. Crochet hooks are available in a wide range of materials, sizes, and shapes; each has advantages and disadvantages of its own.

Material:

Crochet hooks come in a range of materials, such as wood, steel, plastic, bamboo, and aluminum. Your experience with each of these materials will be slightly different. For instance, metal hooks are incredibly quick and smooth, but they can also be chilly to the touch. On the other side, plastic hooks might have more "grip" or friction on the yarn despite being lighter and warmer.

Crochet hooks can also be made of bamboo, resin, or hand-carved wood, among other materials. If you get the chance, experiment with a few different materials to find the kind of hook you most love using.

Shape:

Crochet hooks are available in a variety of forms and shapes. For instance, Boye brand hooks feature a longer shaft with a tapered hook head and throat. Certain brands of hooks have a shorter shaft and an inline-style hook head and throat. In contrast to several other manufacturers of hooks, ergonomic style hooks have a hybrid design that falls somewhere between tapered and inline styles. To identify your preferred style, it's a good idea to try out a few various hooks.

Size:

Of course, there are many sizes for hooks. Your next project's required size will depend on the yarn and pattern you're employing. Use thinner hooks for slender yarns and thicker hooks for yarns that are bulkier. For a decent starting point, look at the yarn label if you're unsure of the hook size to use.

Which kind of crochet hook is ideal for novices?

We advise beginning with aluminum or ergonomic hooks for the majority of novices.

Which size crochet hook is ideal for novices?

To begin, use a mid-sized hook (size H, 5.0 mm) with worsted-weight yarn. Alternatively, purchase a variety pack containing the most popular sizes.

How many hooks are necessary?

You'll need one that is suggested for both your yarn and design to get started. You'll need extra hooks in a range of sizes as your crocheting confidence and proficiency rise.

Crochet hooks are size-specifically branded. However, different regions and nations have various labeling schemes.

Yarn

Choosing yarn for a new crochet project can be one of the most delightful experiences. But choosing the ideal yarn for your next crochet project might be intimidating when you're standing in a yarn store and staring at endless shelves of yarn.

There are lots of various kinds of yarn available for crocheting. It comes in an enormous range of fiber content, weights, colors, and textures.

Texture:

It's wise to use yarns that are simple to work with if you're just starting out—nothing too fluffy, fine, silky, slippery, or bumpy! As your crocheting skills improve, you can practice with textured or delicate fibers.

Color:

A spectrum of hues is accessible in yarn, which includes multicolored, self-striping, and solid yarn. Beginners should begin with lighter-colored yarns to make it easier to see your stitches!

Weight: The yarn weight is divided into seven categories: DK/light (3), superfine (1), fine (2), bulky (5), super bulky (6), jumbo (7), and medium (4), commonly referred to as worsted weight. We suggest choosing bulky or medium-weight yarn when you first start out. It's important to ensure that the hook size and yarn choice match. To determine the recommended hook size, refer to the yarn label on the back or use this crochet hook size reference chart.)

Fiber content: Yarn is available in a wide range of synthetic and natural fibers, including wool, cotton, silk, and acrylic. Since wool and acrylic blend yarns have a little bit more bounce and flexibility than cotton yarns, we suggested using them for learning.

Which kind of yarn works best for crocheting?

We suggest starting with a smooth, medium-weight yarn in a lighter color for your initial projects.

Yarn Needle

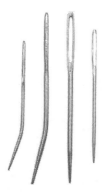

To weave in yarn ends and join crochet pieces, you'll need a yarn needle, which is a large, blunt-tipped needle. Another name for a yarn needle is a darning or tapestry needle.

Size: Yarn needles are available in many shapes, sizes, and materials. Based on the thickness of your yarn, select the appropriate needle size. A yarn needle with a larger eye is necessary when dealing with bulky yarn, for example, in order to facilitate threading.

Shape: Straight or bent-tip yarn needles are offered. Most of my crochet projects are best done using straight yarn needles. However, the bent-tip yarn needles work really well for hooking under the stitch loops. Bent-tip needles come in very handy when assembling amigurumi projects.

Material: Plastic and metal yarn needles are available. For practically all crochet crafts, we like to use metal yarn needles.

Scissors

A sturdy pair of scissors is an essential item for every crocheter's toolbox. Your scissors will be needed to cut yarn and trim ends.

Pretty almost any sharp scissors will work for crocheting. We advise obtaining a tiny pair of scissors that will fit neatly inside your project or crochet bag, if at all possible. These stork scissors or yarn snips are especially adorable.

Stitch Markers

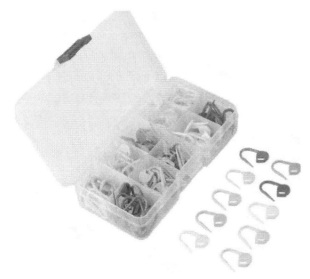

As you crochet, you'll use tiny tools called stitch markers to indicate your stitches. Stitch markers are useful for recording increases and reductions as well as for marking the start and finish of rounds and rows.

Different colors, materials, and shapes are available for stitch markers. Select split ring stitch markers or locking stitch markers for crochet. Avoid purchasing closed stitch markers—they work well for knitting but not for crocheting.

You can also create your own stitch markers using paper clips or bobby pins if money is tight.

Measuring Tape.

A crocheter's tape measure is yet another indispensable instrument. It will be useful for measuring the breadth and length of your crochet creations in addition to your gauge samples.

We advise utilizing a flexible measuring tape, such as this one that retracts. It's sturdy, convenient to wrap around three-dimensional objects, and simple to pack away in your crochet bag.

MORE CROCHET SUPPLIES AND TOOLS

Once you've fallen in love with crocheting, you might want to invest in a few extra accessories and tools to enhance your crocheting experience.

These are some "nice-to-have" crocheting accessories to think about.

Crochet Hook Case

Keeping your crochet hooks organized and stored is a terrific idea with a crochet hook case. It's also a smart approach to store them safely when not in use.

Crochet Project Bag or Tote

Keeping all of your crochet supplies with you is a terrific idea when using a crochet purse or tote. Additionally, it's an excellent location to keep your crochet items that are still in progress, or WIPs.

Yarn Bowl

A yarn bowl is a wooden or ceramic container that you can use to keep your crocheting yarn organized. It's a really useful method for preventing messy, twisted yarn balls.

Row Counter

A tiny tool called a row counter allows you to record how many rows you've completed while crocheting. It is particularly useful for lengthy projects, like as blankets and Afghans.

Hook gauge and Swatch Ruler

We adore using this hook gauge and swatch ruler set to measure my crochet gauge swatches. To find your gauge, use the 4-inch square ruler; to find the size of your crochet hook, use the notches.

Blocking Mats and Pins

Crochet creations are blocked using blocking mats and pins. The process of shaping and drying a crochet creation to achieve the finest possible appearance is called blocking. When finishing crochet creations that look professional, blocking mats and pins might be useful.

Yarn Swift and Ball Winder

Two tools that can be used to wind crochet yarn into balls are ball winders and yarn swifts. To wind yarn into balls without tangling it, use a yarn swift. (The nicest part about balling yarn is that it can help you organize your craft room much more easily.)

You are now ready to begin your crochet journey, knowing what basic supplies and some "nice-to-have" crochet tools you will need!

CHOOSING THE RIGHT YARN

You want to start crocheting, but you're not sure what kind of yarn to use. Learn about the various crochet yarn fibers and weights!

The purpose of these yarn recommendations is to assist novice crocheters in choosing their first yarn to use for practice swatches during their learning process. Almost any type of yarn, including substitute materials that resemble non-fiber yarn, can be used for crocheting. As a novice, though, you'll discover that working with some yarn possibilities will be simpler than others, so it's better to start with them.

Fiber Type

Selecting the kind of fiber to work with is the first choice you must make. Both plant and animal fibers come in an endless variety of possibilities. Everything from banana silk yarn to baby alpaca yarn can be used for crocheting. Nonetheless, wool, cotton, and acrylic yarn are the three types of yarn that novices most frequently choose. Each has advantages and disadvantages, but any will work for novice crocheters.

Wool yarn:

Wool is a great material to practice crochet stitches with. It is a robust fiber that is error-forgiving. Most wool yarns are simple to unravel and reuse if you do make a mistake (in crochet, this is known as frogging). Wool yarn works well for crocheting for most individuals, though some people should be conscious of their allergies.

Cotton yarn:

Since cotton is not as stretchy as wool, crocheting with it can be a little more difficult. (That same characteristic, however, makes it an excellent option for certain tasks when you want the object to maintain its shape!) While some people find cotton a little trickier to work with than wool, the two materials aren't all that different, so you can definitely give it a go as a novice. Cotton yarn is a particularly good option if you're learning to crochet in the summer, when the heat makes working with wool uncomfortable. This is because cotton is lighter than wool.

Acrylic yarn:

All things considered, acrylic is a favorite fiber among crocheters because it is easily accessible, comes in a wide range of colors, and is typically one of the more reasonably priced yarn options. For novices, acrylic yarn is a perfectly good option. One important thing to keep in mind is that some of the less expensive acrylics can be difficult to work with since they have a tendency to split. While uncommon, this can occasionally occur, so if you're new to crocheting with acrylic and finding it difficult, consider trying a different kind of acrylic yarn or yarn made of cotton or wool. Learn to crochet without putting too much pressure on yourself.

Blends:

One of the most widely used kind of crochet yarn is a blend. To develop yarns that incorporate the greatest aspects of both worlds, mills blend several fibers. Do you want a breezy, light yarn for summer? Try using cotton and thin acrylic. I adore alpacas, but the heat is unbearable? A blend of cotton or alpaca and wool would be ideal!

By using blends, mills can also produce unique yarns. Synthetic fibers are frequently used to attach "feature" pieces, such as sequins, to the main yarn strand. Look for blended versions of pricey fibers like cashmere, silk, or wool if you enjoy them because they are frequently less expensive!

Linen:

One of the first fibers ever woven, linen is made from plants called flax. It falls into the featherweight category and is quite robust, with very little elasticity. You may consider it to be a lightweight relative of cotton.

Because of its great absorption capacity, it is suitable for both hot and cold climates. Its lightweight nature makes it an excellent choice for shawls and other items that require good drape.

How will you be able to tell what kind of fiber you're working with, you might be wondering. You'll frequently be able to tell just by looking at or handling the yarn as you become more accustomed to working with different types of yarn. But before that becomes second nature, it's easy to locate the yarn label's indicated type of fiber. To be honest, all the information you require to select the best yarn for crocheting may be found on a yarn label.

WHAT'S THE DIFFERENCE BETWEEN CROCHET WOOL AND CROCHET YARN?

Anything that is 'spun thread used for knitting, weaving, or sewing' is generally referred to as yarn. It also applies to crocheting!

However, wool is yarn that is especially created from sheep, goats, or other similar animals; this is vital to keep in mind if you are concerned about utilizing animal goods.

Yarn vs. Thread

The fiber types we've been talking about so far mostly relate to yarn rather than crochet thread. However, as thread is typically available in cotton or acrylic, the information above covers the essentials. Because yarn is thicker than crochet thread, most people assume that working with it is simpler. Notwithstanding this, there are crocheters who have started using crochet thread right away. Crochet thread is a good place to start for anyone who wants to construct lacy, lightweight objects like tablecloths and doilies with a vintage vibe. If you're not sure which is better—start with yarn and work your way up to threads.

Yarn Weights

What is yarn weight?

When someone refers to anything as "yarn weight," they are referring to the thickness of the yarn strand, not its weight! The terms can be a little deceptive; for instance, 4ply refers to a yarn weight, but a yarn consisting of 4 thread strands spun together is not always a 4ply weight yarn.

Yarn is thicker than crochet thread, as previously indicated. Additionally, there are variations in yarn thickness. We refer to thickness as weight. The weight of the yarn can be found on its label, where it will be numbered 1 through 7 (from the thickest to the thinnest, similar to thick crochet thread). Work with a worsted weight yarn (designated #4 on the yarn label) if you're a novice. This yarn is a nice medium weight. While a "3" (DK weight) is also suitable, some beginners may find it excessively thin. Additionally, a "5" (bulky weight) works well but might not be as simple as worsted weight yarn. But don't be hesitant to experiment with different possibilities; after all, everyone has their own tastes.

Note: Make sure you use the appropriate size crochet hook for the weight of yarn you are using. This size is usually specified on yarn labels in the current era.

TIPS AND CONSIDERATIONS

When searching for a quality yarn to crochet with, keep the following points in mind:

Yarn texture: Stay away from textured yarns and go for smooth ones instead. Avoid using eyelash yarns and other textured novelty yarns for your first few projects since they might be difficult to work with.

Color of yarn: Opt for bright yarn instead of dark; working with dark-colored yarns can make it difficult to see your stitches.

Price of yarn: Yarn prices might differ dramatically between brands and between different fibers. If you're just starting out, it would be wise to use some of the least expensive yarns so you can practice before spending a lot of money. Cotton, wool, and acrylic are therefore excellent fiber options because they are typically the least expensive.

Yardage of yarn: Each ball of yarn has a different amount of yards. This has to do with the cost once more. If you come across two identically priced balls of worsted weight wool yarn, be sure they have roughly equal amounts of yarn in each ball by comparing the yardage.

Yarn color dye lot: Assuming you are using the same color or colorway throughout, you should definitely make sure the colors match if you are crocheting a huge project that calls for multiple balls of yarn. This is the time to check the "dye lot" on the label to ensure that the balls you receive are all from the same dye lot number and don't differ significantly from one another.

Details of washing: If you want to crochet something to wear, it will be vital to follow different washing recommendations for different types of fiber. You can choose wool that shrinks in the dryer and needs to be hand washed and dried flat, or you can use superwash wool that is safe to use in the washer and dryer. This information should be on the label of your yarn.

Ethics and yarn: You can learn a lot about yarn options that are sustainable, organic, vegan, and related to your personal principles regarding animals and the environment. There is a wealth of information available to help you make decisions if this worries you.

You can crochet with any kind of yarn, so don't worry too much about selecting "the perfect yarn" for your first projects. That's the most important thing to know. Enjoy yourself thru it all.

AMERICAN AND ENGLISH MEASURES OF CROCHET AND VARIOUS CROCHET HOOKS'

You might not be aware that crochet hooks come in a wide variety of sizes if you're new to the craft. How do you choose which one to apply to the task at hand? One of the most crucial things to learn when starting to crochet is hook size. Other essentials include selecting the appropriate yarn for your projects and being proficient in the fundamental stitches. Make sure you know how to choose the appropriate crochet hook size because it will impact many parts of your creations.

Relax, we'll cover all you need to know about crochet hook size right here! Let's start by going over the fundamentals of crochet hook size and how to convert US sizes to metric values, along with a useful chart for measuring hook sizes. We'll then discuss the most popular hook sizes and the best hooks for novices to start with.

We will discuss later how to measure your stitches using a crochet swatch and gauge square, as well as how to decide which hook size is best for you. Lastly, we will discuss how to guarantee that you will always have the appropriate crochet hook for your design.

SIZE BASICS

Crochet patterns typically include a suggested hook size to assist you make the pattern as close to the original as possible. The size of a crochet hook corresponds to specific weights of yarn. A hook size, or a range of sizes, that are suggested to work with a specific yarn is also listed on yarn labels.

It's important to note that there isn't a strict standard for crochet hook sizes. Hook sizes have changed independently over time as crochet has developed as a folk art across continents. Both metric and letter measurements can be used to determine the size of a crochet hook. The majority of yarn labels will use one or both kinds of crochet hook measurements, but occasionally you may need to convert the size to ensure that you are using the suggested hook size.

CHART OF CROCHET HOOK CONVERSION FOR THE UNITED STATES AND THE UK

For US and UK crochet hook measurements, see this useful Crochet Hook Conversion Chart.

────────── **Crochet Hook Size Chart (US & UK)** ──────────

Millimeter Size	US Size	Millimeter Size	US Size
2.25 mm	B-1	6 mm	J-10
2.5 mm	--	6.5 mm	K-10½
2.75 mm	C-2	7 mm	--
3.125 mm	D	8 mm	L-11
3.25 mm	D-3	9 mm	M/N-13
3.5 mm	E-4	10 mm	N/P-15
3.75 mm	F-5	11.5 mm	P-16
4 mm	G-6	12 mm	--
4.25 mm	G	15 mm	P/Q
4.5 mm	7	15.75 mm	Q
5 mm	H-8	16 mm	Q
5.25 mm	I	19 mm	S
5.5 mm	I-9	25 mm	T/U/X
5.75 mm	J	30 mm	T/X

Common Hook Sizes

Crochet hooks are available in a variety of sizes, but you will discover that certain hook sizes are more convenient for you to use than others. In terms of normal crochet hooks, the smaller the hook (in US terms) or the smaller the mm size (in UK/metric terms), the smaller the hook. Which crochet hook sizes are most frequently used?

Worst Weight Yarn Hook

H-8 (US) or 5mm (UK) Metric Size

The yarn you'll most likely use when you first start crocheting is worsted weight. The most popular size crochet hook that is suggested for use with worsted weight yarn is the H-8 5mm hook.

Fingering weight yarn hook

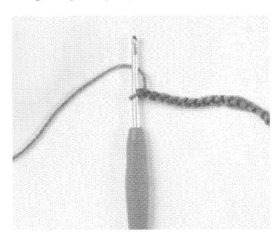

D-3 (US) or 3.25mm (UK) Metric Size

Because worsted weight yarn is smaller than fingering weight yarn, you might want to give it a try after your crocheting comfort level is higher. For fingering weight yarn, try using a D-3 3.25mm crochet hook.

Jumbo yarn hook

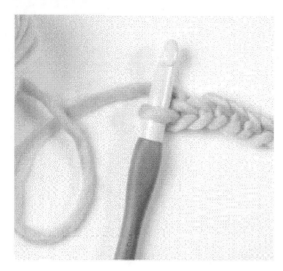

S-35 (US) or 19mm (UK) Metric Size

Use a giant hook, such as an S-35 19mm hook, to crochet roving yarn, huge yarn, cloth strips, rope, or other large yarn. Due to its size, this enormous hook is less frequent, but it is useful if you want to crochet a piece that requires a lot of bulk. Of course, bulky crochet hooks in a variety of other sizes—that aren't nearly as large—can also be used.

Is a Crochet Hook Size A Available?

It's evident from reading the Crochet Hook Size Conversion Chart that there isn't a crochet hook size A. US crochet hook sizes begin at 2.25 mm, or letter B-1, and increase from there. Nonetheless, 2mm crochet hooks are available, indicating that they can be regarded as US size A. On the other hand, based on the crochet hook standards established by the Craft Yarn Council, there technically isn't a crochet hook size A.

How Do Tunisian Hooks Fit?

Tunisian crochet hooks follow the same size specifications shown in the above chart and are measured in the same manner as regular crochet hooks. The only thing that sets Tunisian hooks apart is that their ends are connected with a cord, which makes it possible to carry stitches on the string.

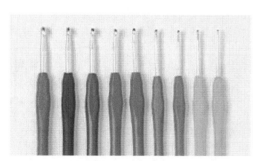
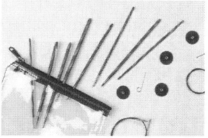

How Come the Size of My Crochet Hook Isn't Labeled?

It might be annoying when crochet hooks are not sized on the label. Older crochet hooks—like the ones you might have inherited from your grandparents—are prone to this. Thankfully, hook sizing has become uniform, allowing us to determine the exact size of any crochet hook!

A knitting needle and crochet hook gauge tool make it simple to determine the hook size. These tiny instruments are bored with holes that are precisely measured in millimeters. To determine the precise size you are working with, simply push your hook into the holes until you locate one that fits. If you like performing both hobbies, these instruments can also be used to measure the size of your knitting needles, which is useful.

Crochet gauge square

A recommended crochet gauge is listed on yarn labels and crochet patterns. What does gauge mean in crochet? It is an approximate measurement in crochet stitches per inch, or square of four inches. You will measure the stitches over a 4 inch portion of your crochet to determine your personal gauge.

When creating a pattern, it is recommended to utilize the stitch pattern you will be using for that project to create a gauge swatch in crochet. While a pattern's recommended gauge often measures 4 inches square, you should measure the middle of the swatch by creating a sample that is roughly 6 inches square. This is because measuring the foundation row or sides will effect how accurate your gauge measurement is.

To obtain the most precise crochet gauge, wash and block your finished swatch in accordance with the yarn or pattern directions. Let the blocked swatch air dry before taking a gauge measurement.

While a crochet gauge square is our preferred gauge measuring tool, a ruler can also be used to determine your gauge. A crochet gauge square is a little square that is used to measure the length of stitches and the degree of tightness or looseness depending on the weight of the yarn and size of the hook.

If you enjoy do-it-yourself projects, you can purchase a gauge swatch ruler that is intended to assist you in determining your gauge or to make your own crochet gauge square, cut a hole in a piece of paper that is 4 inches square.

To utilize a crochet gauge square, place it in the center of your blocked crochet swatch. Next, count the number of rows from top to bottom and the amount of stitches across the 4" To calculate the number of stitches or rows per inch, divide the total number by 4. This figure should line up with the gauge on the yarn label or in the design.

What Happens If My Crochet Gauge Is Off?

Finding the right crochet gauge is especially crucial for items that require a particular size, such as toys, clothes, or accessories. Obtaining the right gauge is especially crucial if your project calls for cables or a complex stitch pattern. Gauge isn't usually as crucial for other crochet projects, such as blankets and afghans, therefore it's acceptable if your gauge measurements are approximate rather than accurate.

If the gauge of your crochet differs, don't freak out! Most crocheters find that their first swatch doesn't match exactly. You can easily adjust your crochet gauge. Try using a larger hook if you find that you are using too many stitches per inch. Use a smaller hook size if the number of stitches per inch is too low.

Don't give up if you need to crochet two or more gauge samples in order to obtain the right gauge. This is merely a step in the crocheting procedure. An hour or two spent on a swatch is preferable than weeks of crocheting a project only to find out it's way too big or little!

Crochet gauge tip:

After figuring out your crochet gauge and getting started, make sure you are staying within the intended gauge by checking your work every few inches with the gauge square.

BASIC CROCHET STITCHES

Learning how to crochet is simple. To start creating a wide range of projects, all you need to know is a few stitches. The six most popular beginner crochet stitches are covered in this chapter along with some useful hints and project ideas.

You'll quickly learn how to create a slip stitch and crochet chain, enabling you to begin simple crafts. Proceed to acquire further fundamental stitches and initiate crafting an assortment of scarves, caps, shawls, and blankets.

CROCHET CHAIN STITCH

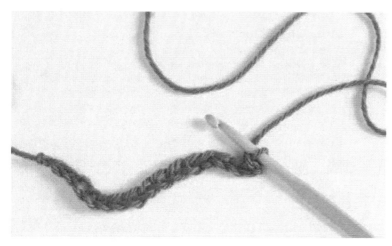

To secure the yarn on the hook and start crocheting, master the slip knot before moving on to the chain stitch. Then master the fundamental chain stitch, which is represented by the pattern letter "ch." Chain stitches are worked in groups of two in the majority of crochet designs; these groupings are called starting chains, base chains, or foundation chains.

Typically, a crochet item begins each new row with a turning chain. The stitches used in that row determine the height of the turning chain, or the quantity of chains you make. For instance, three chains are used to start a double crochet row.

Especially when working in the round, crochet chains are frequently used to join other stitches in a pattern. For instance, a "ch 2" divides double crochet stitches to provide a space in each corner of the traditional crochet granny square pattern.

A popular crochet edging that adds texture by using a crochet chain is called a picot stitch. Crochet chains are a key component of large loops, long fringe, and openwork lace or mesh designs.

Try your hand at a quick creation with a basic crochet chain. Make your first simple crochet scarf by crocheting a set of long chains and tying them at both ends.

CROCHET SLIP STITCH

Small and straightforward, crochet slip stitches. They provide as the basis for all crochet. In a pattern, slip stitch is commonly abbreviated as "sl st." Working in the round is the most common situation in which the slip stitch is used; usually, instructions will say something like "join with a slip stitch to form a ring" or "slip stitch to close round."

For crocheting, slip stitches come in handy when connecting two elements together. One way to join two granny squares together is to slip stitch them next to each other.

For creating flourishes, crochet slip stitches are frequently utilized. Slip stitches, for instance, can be used in surface crochet to give a project's surface color and visual appeal. It's similar to embroidering a flourish on a crocheted object with slip stitches.

SINGLE CROCHET STITCH

Gaining proficiency in the crochet chain and slip stitch provides you with a strong basis upon which to begin crocheting projects. You can crochet many more objects with the single crochet stitch. The single crochet stitch, or "sc," is a common stitch used in patterns.

Short single crochet stitches are used to make thick fabrics. To achieve varied densities, you can adjust the stitch and use different sized hooks or yarn. Once you master the single crochet stitch, you can alter it by working through different loops.

All amigurumi crochet patterns use the single crochet stitch as their foundation stitch. The Japanese craft of amigurumi involves knitting or crocheting tiny plush animals and other three-dimensional objects. For amigurumi crafts, crocheting produces the ideal density of cloth.

HALF DOUBLE CROCHET STITCH

By including an additional step, the half double crochet stitch expands upon the fundamental single crochet stitch. Half double crochet is the height where the single and double crochet stitches meet. The stitch, sometimes known as "hdc," is used in a lot of projects. While the single crochet stitch is a little more closed than this one, the half double crochet still provides enough density to work up cozy objects. Compared to the single crochet stitch, the half double crochet stitch also creates cloth more quickly. When crocheting a job quickly, this stitch comes in handy.

DOUBLE CROCHET STITCH

The "dc," or double crochet, is a versatile stitch that works well with all other fundamental stitches. The foundation of several well-known crochet patterns, including the granny square, filet, and v-stitch patterns, is the double crochet stitch. These patterns give an otherwise simple project a new look by incorporating the fundamental double crochet.

Depending on which loops you go through, you can alter the appearance of the double crochet stitch after you master it. Working in the back loop, for instance, only results in a ribbed pattern that looks good on blankets, cuffs, and hat bands.

TREBLE CROCHET STITCH

In designs, the treble crochet stitch, sometimes referred to as the triple crochet stitch, is shortened to "tr." Though it uses the same basic steps, Compared to the double crochet stitch, the stitch is taller.

The double treble, triple treble, and even taller stitches are just a few of the numerous taller crochet stitches that may be created once you know how to double crochet. With this stitch, you can swiftly increase a project's height. Looser fabric is also produced by taller stitches. Higher stitches are needed for light blankets and open, lacy shawls. looser crochet fabric drapes better and breathes better.

You're well on your way to becoming an extremely skilled crocheter now that you know these six fundamental crochet stitches. Try your hand at creating new stitch designs by combining the fundamental crochet stitches. For instance, the crochet moss stitch mixes single crochet with chains, crochet seed stitch alternates between single and double crochet stitches. Before long, you'll gain the confidence to tackle any basic crochet pattern.

HOW TO HOLD THE CROCHET HOOK.

Although there are many various methods to hold a crochet hook and yarn, crocheters often fall into one of two categories: pencil grippers or knife grippers. Discover the operation of each technique and how to hold a Tunisian crochet hook.

Remember that these are merely the most popular methods of operation when you experiment with these grips. There are many options and modifications, so keep experimenting to find what feels most comfortable for you if something doesn't work for you.

PENCIL GRIP

The "pencil grip" refers to holding your crochet hook in a manner similar to that of holding a pencil or pen. You have the same level of control with the pencil grip as you would when using a paintbrush or a pencil to write or draw.

Usually, the hook in this technique descends into the stitches from above.

Hold the crochet hook in your right hand's thumb, index finger, and middle finger to begin crocheting in the hook pencil technique (see the left-handed variant below). Using your left hand, hold your crochet project and adjust the yarn and tension. You can also hold your crochet project with both hands, using your left hand for part of it and your right hand's pinkie and fourth finger for the remaining portion.

THE LEFT-HANDED CROCHETER'S PENCIL GRIP

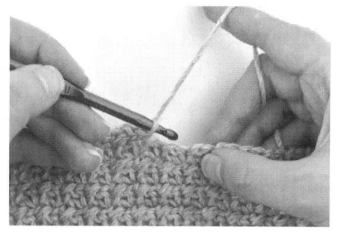

The pencil grip technique is basically the same for left-handed crocheters; it's only inverted. Actually, the image above is the right-handed technique reversed.

Since many left-handed people have slightly varied pencil grips, choose the pencil grip that suits you the best.

THE KNIFE GRIP

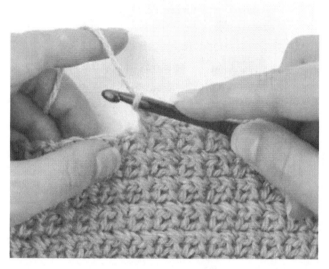

The "knife grip" is like holding a dinner knife when you use it. You have the same level of control using this overhand grip as when using a knife to chop food.Knife grippers frequently assert that their technique is the least taxing on the hands; nevertheless, detractors argue that it lacks the accuracy of the pencil grip. When handling big hooks, even if you usually use the pencil grip, you could discover that the knife grip is more comfortable. The hook usually enters the stitches from below when using this technique. Hold the crochet hook in your right hand, place your hand over it, and use your index finger to guide the hook to make knife-style crocheting. While controlling the yarn and tension, hold your crochet object with your left hand.

THE KNIFE GRIP FOR LEFT-HANDED CROCHETERS

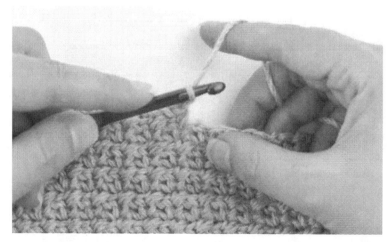

Just like with the left-handed pencil grip, all you have to do is work from left to right and simply flip the knife grip to learn the left-handed version.

Knife grip is preferred by many left-handed crocheters, so try this method and make any necessary adjustments.

HOLDING A TUNISIAN CROCHET HOOK

A traditional crochet hook is not the same as a Tunisian crochet hook, also referred to as an afghan hook or an afghan crochet hook. These hooks lack a thumb rest and are longer in length.

Holding a Tunisian crochet hook with a pencil grip is not the ideal technique. Instead, when crocheting, employ an overhand grip that enables you to control the hook and the work. It resembles a hybrid grip between a pencil and a knife.

Make a loose, easy fist with your working hand when working in Tunisian crochet. The crochet hook must have unrestricted rotation and movement inside the hand. To manipulate the crochet hook and the work-in-progress, including scooting stitches further in either direction on the hook, use your fingers and hand.

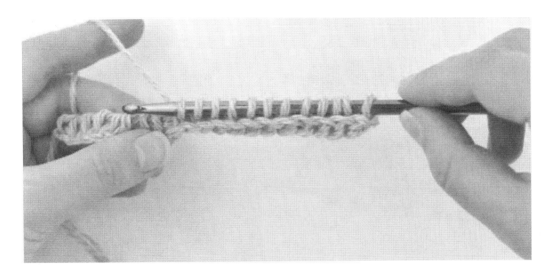

HOLDING A LEFT-HANDED TUNISIAN CROCHET HOOK

Once again, using the flipped image as a guide, invert the grip from the right-handed approach when holding the Tunisian crochet hook in your left hand. Take some time to practice Tunisian crochet, experimenting with different grip sizes to see what works best for you. Before you know it, you'll be crocheting afghans!

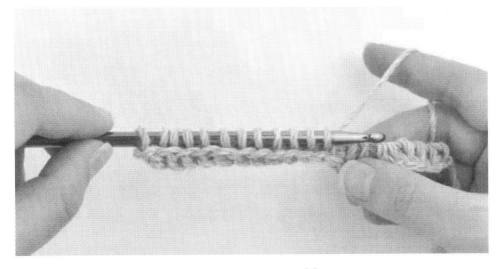

BOOK 2:
CROCHET IN THE ROUNDS, ROW, CHAIN AND PATTERN.

CROCHET IN THE ROUND, ROWS AND MORE.

Making amigurumi successfully requires you to crochet in the round. Let's explore crocheting in the round, distinguishing between the right and wrong sides of your item, and counting and identifying your stitches and rows.

Crocheting can be done in two main ways: spiraling and working in flat rows from side to side. The main method for creating amigurumi is to crochet in the round (spiral).

What Is Crochet In The Round?

There are usually two ways to go to the next round in a crochet design when working in the round: connected rounds and continuous rounds.

Joined Rounds

Using linked rounds is one method of crocheting in the round. To create joined rounds, slip stitch the end of one round before beginning the next. Then, you will normally start a chain 1 at the beginning of each round before beginning your single crochet stitches.

This may be worded like this in a crochet pattern:

R1: Join with a sl st to the beginning after starting with 6 SC in a magic ring. Six stitches

R2: Ch 1, 2 SC in each st around; connect to beginning with sl st. Twelve stitches

R3: Ch 1, connect with a sl st to beginning, 2 SC in next st, 1 SC in next st. Eighteen stitches

Take note of how each round in the sample above begins with a ch 1 and concludes with a slip stitch. This is a useful method for determining if the rounds are connected.

Where your rounds are united, joined rounds will show as a line or seam. In general, this is not the best way to create amigurumi projects.

Continuous Rounds

When creating amigurumi, working in a continuous circle is the recommended way to crochet in the round. This indicates that your round will end without a slip stitch. Rather, you'll keep working your stitches in a spiral pattern.

This may be worded like this in a crochet pattern:

R1: Put six SC in a magic ring to start. Six stitches

R2: Two SC in every circle. Twelve stitches

R3: 1 SC and 2 SC in the following stitch. Eighteen stitches

You'll see that, unlike the linked rounds before, the example above does not use a ch 1 or slip stitch. This is a reliable sign that the rounds are operated nonstop.

At the beginning of the design, there may be a note stating that the pattern is worked in a continuous round, continuous spiral, and/or proposing that you use a stitch marker to keep track of your crochet rounds.

Starting with a magic ring or circle and working your way down a spiral is the usual method for creating a continuous round of crocheting. To avoid sewing a seam when working with amigurumi, it is preferable to work in a continuous spiral as opposed to linked rounds.

Is It Possible to Replace Joined Rounds in a Pattern with Continuous Rounds?

In general, sure! Particularly with plush toys.

A linked circle may be required in some situations, but when dealing with amigurumi, that is usually not the case. This would have relied on each person's unique pattern.

Right Side V. Wrong Side

Knowing which side of your cloth should be facing out is crucial when crocheting in the round since your single crochet stitches won't look the same on both. The "Right Side" is the side that should be seen from the outside, and the "Wrong Side" is the side that will be visible from the inside.

The obvious spiral look indicates which side of your work is the right side. The side of a stitch that faces you while you crochet it is called the right side. The single crochet stitch's right side resembles the letter "V."

The side of a stitch that faces away from you when you crochet is known as the wrong side. The diagonal bar on the back of each single crochet stitch indicates which side is incorrect.

The right side (on the exterior)

Wrong Side (goes on the interior)

COUNTING CROCHET STITCHES

The worst of us are capable of miscounting, forgetting a stitch, or adding too many stitches, therefore you should go back and count your crochet stitches again.

When you look at your crochet project, you may wonder how on earth you're going to know how many stitches it has. After my stitches are worked, how do I count them?

Every single stitch made in crochet will resemble the letter "V." One single crochet stitch makes up each "V." There will be instances where you work two single crochet stitches in the same location, yet each stitch will still have a "V" in it. You can see where we've indicated an area of single crochet stitches in red in the image below.

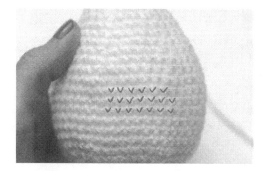

If you wish to count the stitches in the row you're working on, start counting from the top of the stitches. Every single crochet stitch has a front loop and a rear loop at the top of the stitch. Four stitches—red, orange, green, and blue—as well as their top loops may be seen in the picture below.

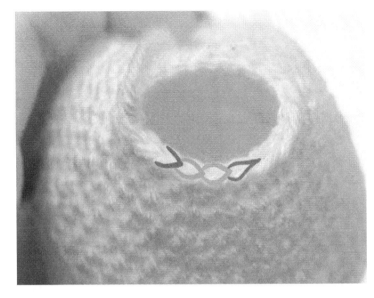

Every line of stitches when working in the round is called a round. A row is one set of stitches when working on a flat item. You may need to count your rounds or rows in each case to make sure you are following the pattern exactly.

Finding the rounds is much simpler after you know how to recognize the single crochet stitches with the "V" shape. A round is made up of one single crochet stitch per line. You will find the magic ring if you begin at the center of your piece. The stitches that were worked in the magic ring are the first round. The exact center of the magic ring is depicted in the picture below by the red dot in the center.

Your second round, the following line of Vs, is located directly above those stitches in the magic ring. Another row of Vs, R3, is directly above that round, and so on.

When crocheting in the round, the row counter is useful. To ensure you don't lose track, all you have to do is hit

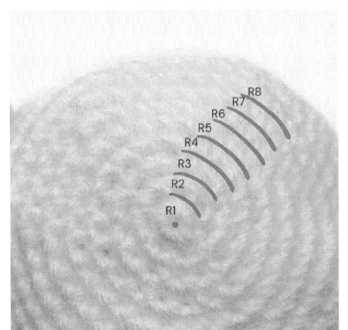

the button on your row counter after finishing a round. In this manner, in the event that you lose count, you won't have to keep counting to figure out which round you just finished or try to mentally recall which round you are on.

As an alternative, you can use tally marks on a piece of paper to record your rounds.

CHAIN STITCH IN CROCHET

In crocheting, chain stitches are essential. Usually, the next stage in a project is to make a chain stitch sequence after creating a slip knot. The rest of the project is constructed using chain stitches as a base. These are among the few fundamental stitches that any novice needs to be familiar with.

Crochet creations frequently have chain stitches strewn throughout the pattern, in addition to the foundation chain. Chain stitches are used in conjunction with other stitches to shape cloth, make stitch patterns, and create spaces between motifs. Simple chains by themselves can be used as ornament hangers, decorative string for fastening presents, and laces for baby booties.

Chain stitches are simple to master, but maintaining the right tension might take some practice.

If you crochet left-handed, flip the hand positions and orientations since these instructions are designed for right-handed crocheters.

How to Hold the Yarn and Hook.

First, secure your hook with a slip knot. Hold the slip knot with your left hand between your thumb and middle fingers using the crochet hook. With the slip knot facing you. The strand that emerges from the ball, known as the working yarn, should pass over your index finger, then between it and your middle finger, across your palm, and back between your ring and little finger. Although it seems strange at first, doing this can help you tension the yarn when you need more from the ball of yarn to form stitches.

Using your fingers, grab the crochet hook in your right hand while holding a pencil., knife, or other comfortable grip.

Keep the crochet hook facing up to begin. Grip the hook loosely enough to allow for easy movement but tightly enough to retain control as you rotate it while creating chain stitches.

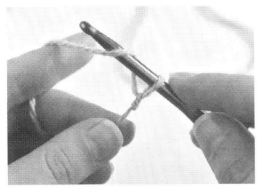

Yarn ahead the Hook

Loop the working yarn around the hook from back to front. To wrap the yarn around the crochet hook, use your left hand to wrap it around from behind and then over the top, or your right hand to manage the hook in the same way. The terms "yarn over" and "yarn round hook" refer to these techniques.

Draw Through a Loop

To prepare the yarn for hooking, turn your crochet hook counterclockwise by about a quarter of a turn. If additional turns are necessary, that's acceptable, but the idea is to make every movement as exact and seamless as you can.

Draw the hook through the loop it is now in and down the hook.

Returning the hook to its original position pointing upwards would probably make it easier for you to finish the stitch as you are just finishing bringing the yarn through.

Making a Chain

That's how you "chained one," or created one chain stitch.

Yarn over hook and drag up loop to start a new chain stitch. As many times as needed, repeat this. Keep your thumb and index fingers a stitch or two away from the loop on the hook as you work your way up the freshly produced chain stitches. When you make your stitches, this will help you maintain greater tension and more control—not too tight, not too loose.

You'll develop a rhythm as you work by turning the crochet hook as you yarn over and back when you draw through a loop. A rhythm facilitates and expedites the procedure.

CHAIN STITCH TIPS

Counting: Usually, the slip knot is not included in the total number of chain stitches needed for the foundation chain of a pattern. The loop on your hook isn't either. Start counting from the first chain stitch you create and stop when you reach the chain that comes before the hook.

Sustain a steady tension: Practice. Hands need practice to pick up new abilities. Your chain stitches should eventually be uniform, smooth, and not overly tight.

Adjust as necessary: There are many various methods to hold the yarn and place the hook when crocheting, and each person crochets a little bit differently. Here are some instructions that show how to do it. You are welcome to change how you work to better fit your needs if this isn't how you feel comfortable.

Never be scared to swap out your hooks: Making your foundation chain with a crochet hook one size larger than the hook you want to use for the remainder of the project may be necessary if you are crocheting with cotton or another non-stretchy yarn. Consider beginning anew with a larger hook for the chain if you feel that your foundation chain is too tight in relation to the first few rows of stitches that come after it.

With strong textiles like wool, this isn't usually essential. To see what will work for your project, make a little swatch.

SLIP STITCH

How to Work and Use Slip Stitch

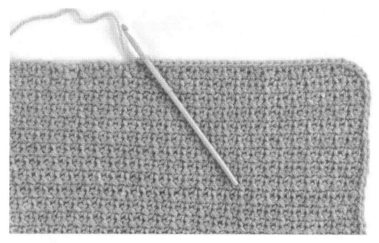

A fundamental crochet stitch that every crocheter has to know is the slip stitch. Knitters can also benefit from it! Slip stitch can be used to complete items with a straightforward border, add ornamental components, and join parts together.

Because slip stitch is shorter than single crochet, it may be used in patterns to work smaller stitches. It's also a very useful and utilitarian stitch.

As you can see above, you can help smooth the edges or hem of a piece and give it a more finished aspect by adding slip stitch edging to your project. While doing this in matching yarn is usual, it's also fun to provide a pop of contrast!

Almost anytime after you start a project, you can work a slip stitch.

Place your crochet hook into the desired slip stitch stitching location if it already has an active loop on it. After that, hook your yarn as shown.

Pull Yarn Through

Drag the yarn through your project from above.

Complete the Slip Stitch

Lastly, pass the recently formed loop through your hook's active loop. After a few attempts, these steps practically form one motion.

Now that the slip stitch is finished.

JOINING A CROCHET ROUND OR MAKING A RING

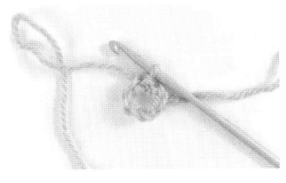

Forming a Ring

Some designs, like granny squares or hexagon patterns, start with a ring in the middle. These patterns usually begin with a few chain stitches joined together to form this ring; the join is made with a slip stitch.

All you have to do is slip stitch and put your hook into the end of the beginning chain to form a ring.

Joining a Round

Slip stitch can be quite helpful when crocheting in rounds. Upon completion of a round, there may be a large gap between the starting and ending points of the round. In a round, a slip stitch can be used to bridge the space between the start and end stitches. When creating granny squares, for instance, this is typical.

If you are following a pattern, it will indicate whether or not to do this. In certain situations, like as when working your rounds in a continuous spiral, it may not be required to sew a slip stitch at this point.

SLIP STITCHES IN SURFACE CROCHET

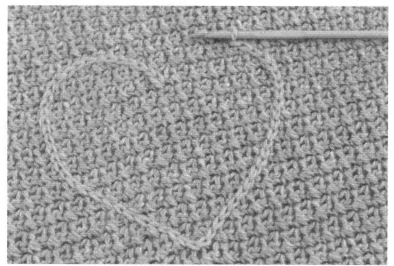

Any surface that you can pierce with a crochet hook can be worked in slip stitch, including the majority of knitted and crocheted materials. This is useful for adding flair to your knitting and crocheting creations.

Slip stitch can be used to add decorations using just the slip stitch or to outline forms or designs that have been created with color changes in your work. Try using slip stitch, for instance, to add names or initials to your knitted or crocheted items. It's like using yarn instead of embroidery to embellish anything knitted or crocheted!

You can cut out a paper shape, pin it in place, and then slip stitch around it to mark the designs. Alternatively, you can outline the pattern or letters with a vanishing ink pen. Make sure to try it first on a swatch to see whether the markings will show through.

MORE WAYS TO USE SLIP STITCH

Slip-stitching Crocheted Elements Together

To link elements, slip stitches are a fantastic option. This stitch can be used, for instance, to bind off crochet squares or to hem sweater sleeves or shoulder seams. Slip stitch is a wonderful option if you're looking to join something else.

When doing each slip stitch to join two sections together, pass your hook through both pieces or edges.

Sometimes a slip stitch edging helps when whip stitching items together. When joining the elements, working a slip stitch edge gives you a clear spot to lay each whip stitch.

It's crucial to count your slip stitches and work exactly the same amount of stitches around each square while working a slip stitch edging around clusters of afghan squares. This will help to ensure that your whip stitching runs smoothly.

Apart from its utility as an edge, join, or decorative stitch, slip stitch can also be worked in flat rows or rounds like any other crochet stitch. Bosnian crocheting, also known by a number of other names, is the process of crocheting a cloth using the slip stitch that results in a denser material.

SINGLE CROCHET

One of the most crucial stitches to master if you want to learn to crochet is single crochet, or simply sc. Single crochet stitches are used in the majority of crochet patterns and crafts.

One of the simplest stitches to learn is single crochet, sometimes known as double crochet in British crochet patterns. There are numerous applications for the single crochet stitch once you've mastered it. It can be worked in spirals, rounds, or rows as an edging to provide a variety of effects, or it can be combined with other stitches to create an endless number of combinations.

Insert Your Crochet Hook

After creating the foundation chain of stitches, insert the hook into the first chain. For the second row and thereafter, insert your hook into the single crochet stitch in the row immediately below it.

Underneath each of the chain's two loops, slide the hook.

You may view samples of these patterns at the end of the tutorial. Some patterns need you to work through only one of the loops, which produces a different effect. If in doubt, run both loops through.

Yarn Over and Grab the Yarn

Now that the crochet hook is in position, get ready to create a loop. Grasp the yarn with your crochet hook after wrapping it around it.

You may discover that you reach a point where the first and second steps flow seamlessly from one another once you've rehearsed them to the point of automaticity. As soon as you put the yarn into the stitch, your hook will catch it.

Draw up the Loop

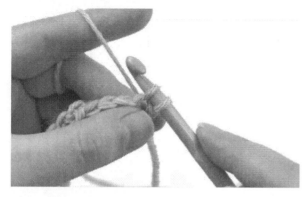

Working the yarn through the loops, pull or "draw" the hook. At this point, your hook ought to have two stitches, or "loops."

Yarn Over Again

Hook the yarn by re-wrapping it around your crochet hook.

Insert the Yarn Into Both Loops.

Pull the yarn and hook through the hook's two loops. The single crochet stitch is finished now. Your crochet hook has one loop left on it. The beginning of your next stitch is this loop.

To add more single crochet stitches across the row (or round), you can repeat these procedures as many as necessary.

TIPS FOR BEGINNERS

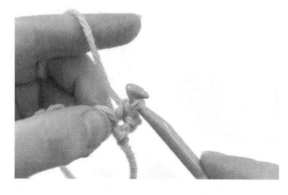

Beginning crocheters may find the first row particularly difficult if they are crocheting in rows. Since there isn't much to grip at first, holding the work might be challenging for many new crocheters.

Ask a more seasoned crocheter to work the first few rows of a single crochet stitch for you if you are having problems. After that, you can keep crocheting on the same item. It will get easier to hold the work after you've finished the first few rows.

You'll find it much easier to work those challenging first rows in subsequent projects once you've completed enough rows to become proficient in the single crochet stitch.

Things You Can Make Using Just One Crochet

The stitch looks different if you attempt threading your hook through just one loop. Try these modifications, which match the picture's quadrants:

Top Left: Pass the hook through the stitch's two loops. That is the typical stitch used in single crochet. This is what people mean when they speak to "single crochet" in the absence of any further explanation.

Top Right: Only the front loop (FLO) of the stitch should have the hook inserted. This version produces a single crochet that is more open in style.

Bottom Left: Place the hook solely into the stitch's back loop (BLO). This results in a variety that seems ribbed. When the fabric is finished, it also has some elasticity to it.

Right bottom: Thread the hook through loops that alternate (FLO, BLO, FLO, BLO, etc.). This produces a crochet fabric with a lot of texture.

To finish the single crochet, just follow the same procedures wherever you decide to insert your crochet hook. For products you wish to be closed (instead of frilly), the dense, thick fabric produced by all these variations of single crocheting is ideal. Single crochet is a great stitch for making scarves, gloves, thick blankets, and washcloths.

You can create a plethora of items once you master single crocheting. For example, single crochet is the main stitch used in amigurumi and is also employed in other kinds of crochet creations.

HALF DOUBLE CROCHET STITCH (HDC)

Half double crochet stitches are lovely basic stitches that any novice should learn. This tutorial provides instructions on how to work with the half double crochet (HDC) stitch and how to use it in projects. Learning HDC is a logical next step for novices who have already mastered single and double crochet.

HDC is shorter than double crochet but taller than single crochet, as the name implies. It is related to the two fundamental stitches and is a foundational crochet stitch. A tiny modification results in a smaller height and a distinct third loop.

Instructions

Choosing Yarn and a Crochet Hook

You can work with any yarn and any crochet hook to complete half double crochet tasks because this stitch appears in a wide variety of projects. Should you be utilizing a crochet design, the pattern will specify the precise materials required.

In the event that you are not following a pattern, determine the hook size required for the yarn by selecting it and consulting the yarn label. As a nice place to start, beginners might choose to attempt a worsted weight yarn and size H crochet hook.

A smooth, light-colored worsted-weight yarn is a wonderful option when learning new crochet stitches.

Crochet a Foundation Chain

A slip knot is the first step in any crochet creation.

Create a base chain into which the first row will be worked. A starting chain, or foundation chain, can have any length. Use the chain length called for in the crochet pattern if you are using one.

Start in the Correct Chain

Three chains distant from your hook is the chain you will crochet into to begin the first half double crochet into the foundation chain.

A turning chain is used to start a row in crocheting. The height of the crochet stitch determines the height of the turning chain. Make a turning chain in half double crochet by chaining two.

Pull Yarn Over and Place Crochet Hook Inside

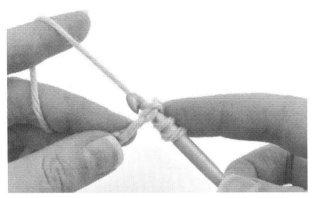

Let's create the first HDC now. Pull the yarn taut, then slide the crochet hook through the stitch.

Keep in mind that you would also complete this step if you were creating a double crochet stitch. You wouldn't yarn over before putting the crochet hook in if you were doing a single crochet stitch. The stitch is taller than a single crochet because of the height added by the yarn over.

Pull Through and Yarn Over the Stitch

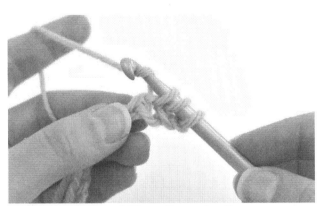

Pull the yarn through the stitch and repeat the yarning process. Three loops ought to be on the hook at this point.

Pull Through and Yarn Over the Loops

Yarn over after putting the yarn through each of the three loops.

The first half double crochet stitch is now finished.

Complete the Row

Work through the foundation chain row and all the stitches in each succeeding row, repeating the procedures for every HDC.

Turn the work to start the new row, then chain two to create a turning chain. Create HDC stitches in the subsequent stitch as well as in every stitch from the previous row.

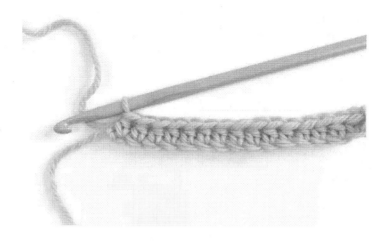

In half double crochet, increase and decrease

Any HDC design that is performed in consistent rows can be crocheted using the fundamental half double crochet stitch. However, you might need to understand how to increase and decrease in half double crochet for patterns that include shaping.

How to Increase HDC

Simply make an additional half double crochet stitch where you have previously made one to increase. You may learn where and how to do this using crochet designs. For instance, instead of working just the final stitch, crochet two HDC stitches at the end of the row to increase.

How to Decrease HDC

It's a little different, but still simple, to decrease. How to do it is as follows:

Pull the yarn taut and thread the hook through the stitch as usual.

Twirl around and carry on as usual.

After you've yanked, work the hook into the following stitch.

As indicated here, yank through five loops on the hook and yarn over.

Pull through all five loops and yank over.

The decreasing stitch creates a single stitch by working over two successive stitches and joining them at the top. It may be shortened to dec HDC (decrease half double crochet) or HDC2tog (half double crochet two together).

TIPS FOR WORKING WITH HALF DOUBLE CROCHET IN DIFFERENT MANNERS

Half double crochet is a word used in American crochet; in UK crochet designs, it is known as half treble crochet.

In many patterns, the double crochet stitch can be swapped out for a half double crochet stitch to create a shorter but same design. Alternatively, you might create an HDC v-stitch instead of a regular v-stitch.

Blanket edgings can be made with half double crochet shell stitches.

Working in Different Loops

A simple stitch such as half double crochet can be made to seem different by working into one loop alone, rather than both. For a ribbed design, half double crochet looks fantastic when worked exclusively into the back loop, but you may also work into the front loop.

Because of the way half double crochet is made, there is a third loop. This means that in order to ensure that you are crocheting into the front or back loop correctly, you need to gain a deeper understanding of the anatomy of the loops. Additionally, it implies that you can work into the third loop as an alternative, which is a terrific way to get a knit-like fabric.

DOUBLE CROCHET STITCH

One of the fundamental stitches you will learn when you first start crocheting is the double crochet stitch. It's a really adaptable stitch that you may use in many different ways as you progress with crocheting. This article explains how to make the double crochet stitch first, then goes over double crochet variations and uses for the dc stitch. You might be shocked to see how many things you can accomplish with this crochet stitch, even if you are an experienced crocheter!

Begin With Your Foundation Chain

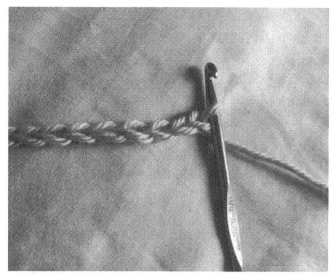

Unless you opt to construct a chainless foundation double crochet, which is covered later in this section, you will need something to work your double crochet stitches into. It is therefore necessary for you to start by crocheting a foundation chain.

Tie a slip knot first.

Next, work your chain into a crochet. Should you be utilizing a crochet design, the pattern will specify the length of your foundation chain.

If you are not using a pattern, you will add two more stitches to the chain you crochet after it reaches the desired length for your item. For illustration, suppose you wish to make a slender scarf with ten double crochet stitches across. Make a 10 + 2 (or 12) foundation chain.

You add the extra chains because, as you shall see in a moment, those will count as the first double crochet.

Yarn over and thread hook through chain

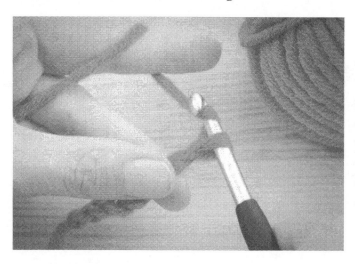

Slide the hook into the chain after tugging it over. On this first stitch, you will hook onto the third chain from your hook. Though you won't realize it until you've done the next stitch, the chains you're skipping serve as your first double crochet of the row. However, because they help in the production of the chains that comprise the first double crochet, you add those extra chains to the foundation chain as previously stated.

For the time being, however, you may simply assume that this is how it's done, so yarn over and place the hook into the third chain from the hook.

Yarn Over Again and Pull Through

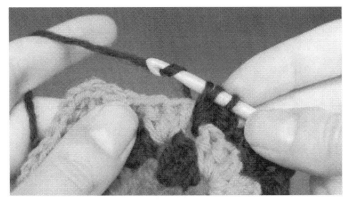

After re-knitting, draw the yarn through the third chain from the hook you originally used. You should notice three loops on your crochet hook after completing this step.

Pull through and yank over two loops on the hook.

Repeatedly yank. Using your hook, pull the yarn through the first two of the three loops. At the end of this stage, there will be two loops remaining on the hook.

Yarn Over and Complete the Stitch

For one last time, yank over. Take care to pull through the two loops that remain on the hook. The double crochet stitch is finished.

To summarize, the double crochet stitch is:

- Distressed beyond measure.
- Put the hook into the stitch where the double crochet should be placed.
- Repeatedly yarn.

- Make it through.
- Repeatedly yarn.
- Grab the first two of the three loops on the hook.
- Repeatedly yarn.
- Thread the last two loops through the hook.

47

That's the only thing about it. Having skipped the first three chains, which are the first double crochet stitch of the first row, you made the first double crochet stitch. should stand to the right of what now looks to be another double crochet stitch once you've finished the first one.

This section's "to the right" instructions are meant for crocheters who work from the right side of their body. For crocheters who are left-handed, it will be the opposite.

Finishing the Double Crochet Stitches Row

Only the first three chains at the start of the foundation row need to be skipped. There's no need to skip chains after that. For your next double crochet, you will therefore follow the identical instructions as before, but instead of inserting the hook into the previous stitch, you will do it immediately to the left of the double crochet hook. Until the conclusion of the row, you will continue adding one double crochet stitch to each chain.

Turning Chain of 3

As said in step six, to produce the project's initial double crochet, you don't need to skip any chains other than the foundation chain at the beginning. But, you do need to make a turning chain each time you flip the piece and start a new row. It is comparable in that you are creating the row's first double crochet without actually doing the double crochet stitch's steps. Chain three to do this. This will be considered your row's first double crochet. The next double crochet is worked by turning your yarn over and working the stitch into the subsequent stitch.

Working just in the front and back loops

The instructions for crocheting rows of double crochet stitches are provided above. But you may play around a lot with the double crochet stitch to make slightly different motifs. Firstly, you can crochet your stitches into the back loops or the front loops of each row separately. This will use the same fundamental double crochet stitch to create a variety of textures, tensions, and ribbing possibilities.

See what happens when you work double crochet in a variety of loops.

Increasing and Decreasing

You will most likely need to adjust your stitches if you wish to crochet anything other than squares or rectangles.

Simply crochet two double crochet stitches into one stitch from the row below to increase double crochet.

Essentially, you have to combine two successive stitches into one when decreasing double crochet. Here's how to use double crochet for that:

As usual, start the double crochet stitch. Before you complete the last yarn over, you will repeat all of the stages until there are only two loops remaining on the hook.

Keep the work exactly as it is on the hook. Next, insert the hook into the stitch after yarning over. Proceed as you normally would, pulling through the first two loops on the hook, yarn over, pull through, and repeat once more.

There should be three loops on the hook. Yarn over and pull the yarn through all three loops. By securing them with a common thread at the top, this essentially converts the two side-by-side double crochet stitches into one double crochet stitch to work into in the next row.

Chainless Foundation for Double Crochet

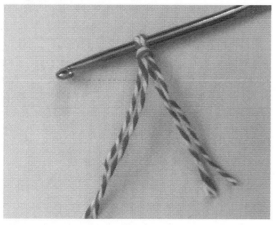

As said in the first stage of this tutorial, you can really start crocheting without actually creating a foundation chain. The foundation chain is essentially worked into the double crochet stitches all at once. This is a method for starting crochet projects that is more complex. Because chainless foundation stitches are more uniform than stitching into a chain, many people prefer them.

Double Crochet Around Posts

The usual practice for crocheting is to work into the top of the stitches from the row below. They can, nevertheless, also be made to go around the posts. Post stitches made with double crochet are a popular choice. They are frequently used to create cables and fabrics with intricate textures. Once you have mastered front post double crochet and back post double crochet, you can move on to more complex methods like fpdc2tog.

The following describes how to do a front post double crochet stitch:

Yarn over.

To crochet around a circumstance, insert your hook through your work from front to rear such that the post is "front" of your hook.

Continue to yank and persevere. Your hook will have three loops on it. At this stage, you will follow standard double crochet procedures.

Pull through the first two of the hook's three loops by yanking over.

Pull through the last two loops on the hook and yank over.

The technique for working a back post double crochet is the same as for doing a front post double crochet, except you would put the hook from the back of the work into the front work around the desired stitching position.

Techniques That Use Double Crochet Stitches

Worked in the above mentioned ways, basic double crochet stitches can be used to create a wide variety of objects. However, once you understand how to double crochet, the world truly opens up to you because double crochet stitches are used to create a plethora of the greatest traditional designs and beloved techniques.

The double crochet stitch is used in the following techniques:

The traditional granny square to crochet: A granny square is constructed from three double crochet stitches in each cluster. Knowing how to work in the round and crochet chains is all that's required for this project.

Other forms for granny crochet: Granny rectangles, triangles, and circles are also made with the double crochet.

Filet crochet: With patterns ranging from early vintage designs to the most modern, this fantastic crochet subgenre lets you create letters and other amazing visuals. Chain gaps and double crochet stitches are used in its construction.

V-stitch: Another crochet design that combines double crochet stitches with crochet chains is the v-stitch. "V" forms are made by the arrangement of the chains and stitches. This is a very common option for a 21st-century pattern.

Crossed double crochet: The crossed double crochet (xdc) creates an x-shaped pattern in contrast to the v-shaped pattern made by the v-stitch. It's a fairly easy method to make crochet cloth that appears more complicated than it is to do.

Cluster stitch: A variety of fundamental stitches can be used to work clusters, bobbles, and popcorn stitches, but the double crochet stitch is frequently used.

Crochet shell stitch: Similar to other shell stitches, this one is most frequently produced in double crochet. However, it can be made in any height.

V-stitch crochet shell: This is a combination of the dc shell and dc v-stitch.

Simple mandala: Mandalas constructed with crochet can be created with an endless variety of stitches. Nonetheless, a straightforward favorite—the conventional 12-round crochet mandala—completely depends on double crochet stitches.

TREBLE CROCHET

One essential basic crochet stitch that you'll probably require for working with a variety of crochet patterns is the treble stitch. Another name for it is triple crochet. It is somewhat taller than a double crochet stitch, but otherwise comparable.

Trebles can be paired with other stitches to create fascinating stitch patterns, just like any other fundamental stitch. They can be worked into many various configurations, such as rows, squares, circles, triangles, and other shapes, and used in a multitude of ways.

You will first learn how to work a treble crochet stitch in this part. Then you will also learn how to work in rows with treble crochet. The crochet pattern is designed for the right hand only. If you are left-handed, you will work across the rows from left to right by flipping the direction.

Guide to Treble Crochet

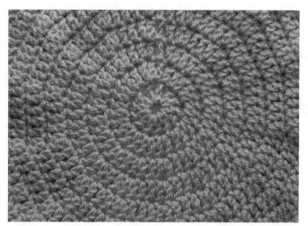

A fundamental crochet stitch is the treble crochet. The method of work is nearly identical to that of a double crochet stitch.

But, you'll yarn over a bit longer at the start, enabling you to make a stitch that's marginally taller than double crochet. The analogous differences between double and treble crochets will be clear to you if you already know how single and double crochets differ from one another.

Almost any yarn or crochet thread can be used to perform treble crochet. Either rows or rounds can be worked on it.

Treble Crochet Stitch Instructions

Start by crocheting a chain to begin. Do you still know how to do a chain stitch? You will start by crocheting a sequence of chain stitches in order to work the treble crochet stitch in rows.

Alternatively, you might begin by crocheting your treble stitches straight onto fabric; here's another option. Alternatively, incorporate them into a composition that you've already started. If that is your preference, you can work your treble crochet into the next stitch without working through the initial chain.

Your initial treble crochet stitch will be the first four chain stitches you make. You should work into the fifth chain from your crochet hook when you crochet the following stitch.

Twice wrap the yarn around your crochet hook.

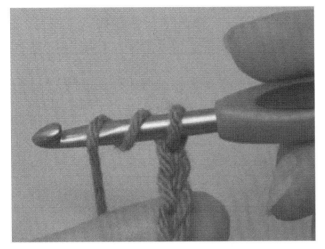

Take your yarn and wrap it around your crochet hook twice to start the next treble crochet stitch. Together with the active loop you already had, there will be three loops on the hook.

Work Into the Fifth Chain

The initial treble crochet stitch is made up of the first four chains from your hook. so you'll skip those and hook onto the fifth chain stitch instead. The crochet hook head is visible in the image on the left, directly next to the location where the hook will be inserted to complete the stitch.

Treble Crochet Stitch in Progress

When your hook is in the sixth chain stitch, it will look like this. This simply carries over from the last step.

Working on a Treble Crochet Stitch: Getting Yarn

Next, use your hook to grip the yarn. Put another way, goof around.

Working on a Treble Crochet Stitch: Getting Through

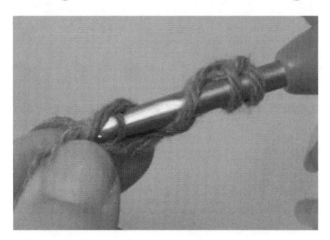

Pull it through the chain stitch at this point. The combination of steps six and seven is often referred to as "yarn over, pull through."

Four Loops on the Crochet Hook

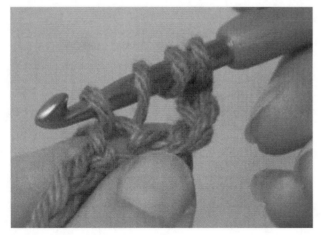

At this stage in the task, you should have four loops on your crochet hook.

Working on a Treble Crochet Stitch - Wrapping Yard

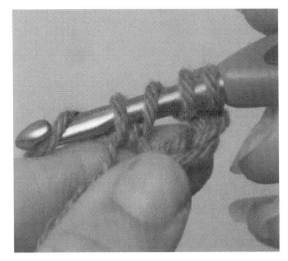

Rewind step six by wrapping the yarn around your hook.

Working on a Treble Crochet Stitch: Pull Loops

and draw it through your hook's initial two loops. If you have already learned how to work a double crochet stitch, you will be accustomed to pulling through only two loops.

Treble Crochet Stitch in Progress

Three loops will remain on the hook in the end. You'll note that there will be one less loop on the hook than the previous time when you follow the instructions to finish the stitch.

Treble Crochet Stitch in Progress – Wrapping

Re-encircle your hook with the yarn.

Treble Crochet Stitch in Progress

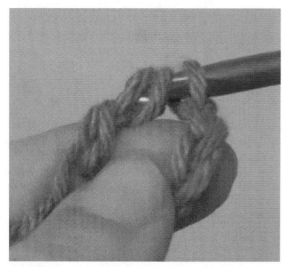

and draw it through the hook's following two loops. Put another way, go through steps six and seven once more.

Treble Crochet Stitch in Progress

There will be two loops left on the crochet hook after this. By now, you should be starting to understand how this stitch is put together.

Treble Crochet Stitch in Progress

Once more, wrap the yarn around the crochet hook.

Treble Crochet Stitch in Progress

and draw it through your hook's final two loops. Put another way, finish the stitch by going through steps six and seven one last time.

The Completed Treble Crochet Stitch

This is the finished treble crochet stitch. You will see that there is now just one loop left on your hook. We refer to this as your "active loop."

A Row of Treble Crochet Stitches

You will work your way through the chain stitches in your starting chain, one complete treble crochet stitch at a time, by repeatedly repeating the previous steps.

Here's an example of a completed row of treble crochet stitches once you've worked your way across the entire row.

Crochet Your Turning Chain

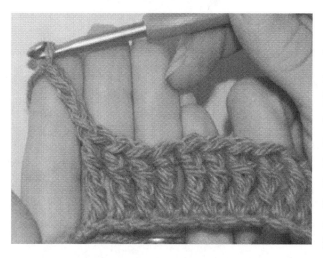

Turning chain work is the next phase. A treble crochet stitch typically has a turning chain of four stitches, therefore between each row of treble crochet stitch, you will work four chain stitches. This is just a suggested amount of chain stitches that works well for most crocheters in typical situations; it's not an exact quantity. Feel free to work a turning chain that is longer or shorter as desired. There are several justifications for wanting to. Naturally, you should adhere to the directions provided in your crochet pattern if it calls for a different starting chain number.

Turning the Work

The next step is to construct your new row of stitches on top of the previous row of treble crochet stitches by working back across the row. You will need to transfer your work to the other side in order to achieve this goal. It will resemble the image that was shown above.

Another Treble Crochet Stitch

Over the top of the stitch you worked in the previous row, you will create another treble crochet stitch. After wrapping the yarn around the hook twice, slide the hook under the two loops of the stitch that was created in the row below it, wrap the yarn around once more, and pull the loops through one at a time until the stitch is finished.

You may simply keep going through those processes again and again until the piece is as lengthy as you would like it to be.

Naturally, you can work treble crochet into one loop only (either the front or back loop) to create a variety of design effects, just like with other fundamental crochet stitches. In the event that your crochet pattern specifies differently, you will complete both loops.

Treble Crochet Stitch Worked in Rows

Cut the yarn after you're done, leaving a long tail for weaving in the ends. Next, insert the cut yarn tail into the active loop and give it a firm tug. If desired, you can then weave in your ends.

You can view a picture of the completed treble crochet stitch cloth at the left.

MAGIC LOOP.

The magic circle technique might be just what you need the next time you begin a crochet project with a round center to keep it closed and taut. This technique, often known as the magic loop or magic ring, works well for amigurumi creations. It's also useful for beginning granny squares and other designs that begin with a circle.

A few chain stitches are often linked to form a ring at the beginning of projects with a circular center or starting point. Next, stitch the first round of stitches onto the ring's center. This is effective, but it has a tiny gap in the middle.

You can shut that opening by pulling the yarn's end like a drawstring using the magic circle. In fact, you can normally use more stitches in that initial round than you would with a standard ring, depending on the yarn you're working with.

A lot of patterns specify when to use a magic circle, but you can experiment with other projects that don't call for it. It's okay if the outcomes seem a little different. The magic crochet circle instructions are provided here. These patterns illustrate the right-handed technique using words used in American crocheting. If you crochet with your left hand, invert the initial loop construction and continue the tutorial using left-handed movements, working clockwise.

Instructions

Make a Loop in the Yarn End

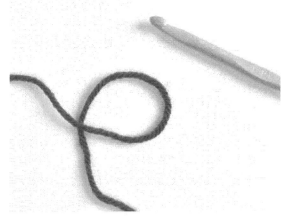

The yarn's end should be looped into a lowercase "e". The loose end should be crossed by the yarn coming from the skein.

To ensure you're prepared to move on to the next stage, it would be helpful to keep this in your hand while you complete this initial loop.

With the working yarn remaining on top of the yarn end, flip this to a reverse e if you are left-handed.

Insert the Hook in the Circle

Place the hook in the center of the yarn circle, holding the loop in place. From back to front, wrap the working yarn around your hook. This is precisely the same as any other yarn.

Draw the Yarn Through the Circle

The loose circle can make this feel a little strange at first. As you pull up the yarn loop, grasp the point where the circle crosses and it will hold.

Yarn Over to Start a Chain Stitch

Holding the yarn circle, continue creating a rotating chain.

Twirl from front to rear.

Complete the Chain Stitch

To finish a chain stitch, draw the hook through the loop on the hook.

One chain stitch is all that is needed for this first turning chain because this lesson demonstrates how to begin a magic circle using single crochet stitches. Should you be commencing with alternative stitches, utilize the quantity of chains required for a turning chain in that particular stitch size.

Insert the Hook and Start a Single Crochet

You can now begin working with your first single crochet stitch.

Draw up a loop by inserting the hook into the center of the ring, yarn over, and knit.

Complete the First Single Crochet

To complete the single crochet stitch, yarn over and draw yarn through both loops on your hook.

Your yarn starting circle should now feel a little more stable. Make sure not to tug at the loose end while working, since it can still pull and move.

Add More Single Crochet Stitches to the Circle

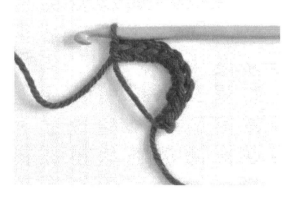

Work the number of stitches required to complete the pattern. It's alright if the ring is quite open.

Join the Ring of Stitches

To begin tightening the ring, pull the end of the yarn. This closes the distance between the final stitch and the turning chain.

Utilizing a slip stitch, join the circle.

Pull the Yarn End to Close the Magic Circle

Pull the end till the circle is as tight as you would like it to be to complete the closure.

This method makes it feasible to loosen the center while simultaneously enabling you to tighten the center. Make sure the yarn is securely fastened at the end to prevent your work from opening up as you use it.

READING CROCHET PATTERNS.

You can begin the enjoyable process of making your favorite projects as soon as you understand how to read crochet instructions! We'll walk you through the most often used terminology, acronyms, and pattern details so you can start crocheting right away if you're having trouble understanding how to read a crochet pattern.

How do you read a crochet pattern?

Reading written crochet patterns can feel like reading a foreign language when you're initially learning the craft. But you'll be stitching away in no time if you get the terminology. To begin, all you'll need to know is a few popular crochet terminology and symbols, along with a few fundamental stitch abbreviations.

Acquiring Knowledge of the Crochet Language

Learning basic crochet terminology is the first step towards being able to read a written crochet pattern. You'll use these terms frequently after you grasp them.

BASIC STITCH ABBREVIATIONS

The most popular crochet stitches that you may come across in crochet patterns have the following abbreviations. Once you learn to read them by heart, you'll notice that these acronyms make patterns easier to understand and shorter.

- Ch: stands for chain
- Sl st: stands for slip stitch
- Sc: stands for single crochet
- Hdc: stands for half double crochet
- Dc: stands for double crochet
- Tr: stands for treble crochet

The most typical stitch acronyms you'll come across are these ones. You won't necessarily need to recall every stitch name because many patterns will remind you of them as you work.

Common Crochet Terms

You'll find certain abbreviated phrases that are frequently used in crochet patterns in addition to fundamental stitch abbreviations. The definitions of the terms you'll frequently encounter are listed here.

- Inc: stands for increase (create a stitch or stitches).
- Dec: stands for reduce, meaning to remove a stitch or stitches.
- Join: fuse two stitches together (a slip stitch is typically used for this).
- Turn: turn your work over to begin working on a new row of stitches.
- Rep: stands for repeat
- Sp stands for space, and it describes crocheting in the space or gaps between stitches.
- St: stands for thread or stitches (St/Sts)
- Chain Space stands for (Ch-Sp)

Parentheses, Brackets, and Asterisks

Finally, a few distinct symbols are used in crochet patterns to indicate how to work the design. Your pattern may have asterisks, parentheses, and brackets.

Parentheses and brackets in crochet patterns

Parentheses () are frequently used to indicate a collection of stitches that need to be done together. As an example:

Row 4: (2 sc, ch 3, 2 sc) in the next sc

This indicates that all of the stitches enclosed in parenthesis would be combined into a single crochet stitch.

As in the example below, parentheses can also be used to show how many times a set of stitches is repeated.

Row 9: Sc in the next 3 sc, ch 1, (sc in the next dc, ch 4, sc in the next dc) 4 times, ch 1, sc in the next 4 sc

The pattern included in parenthesis would be repeated four times in this row, and then the next four sc would be the ch 1, sc.

Generally speaking, brackets [] and parentheses are used in very similar ways. They can often be used in place of one another. However, brackets are typically used to group stitches that need to be repeated.

Before proceeding to the next stage, the steps in the example below that are enclosed in brackets must be completed seven times.

[ch 2, sc in ch 3 sp] 7 times

Asterisks in crochet patterns: How to Read Them

Finally, a sequence of repeated stitches or actions are indicated by asterisks (*). This lessens the need to repeatedly write out the same processes.

First, let's look at a basic example of using an asterisk:

Sc in the chain after the hook. All stitches in a row should be sc. Turn at the finish of row one of chain. Repeat from * to * until the required width is achieved.

This straightforward example can frequently be seen in a project where you can customize the size, such a dishcloth or potholder.

Here's another instance of using an asterisk:

Round 3: First Ch. * 2 sc into the following stitch. Just one SC. In the next stitch, work 2 sc. From * to the finish, repeat. Sl to join. (18 stitches)

To complete the row, you will merely need to keep repeating the pattern "one single crochet, two single crochet in the next stitch" in this example.

Sometimes a pattern will use both one asterisk (*) and two asterisks (**), as in the following example:

Ch 5, *rep from * twice, from * to ** once again, connect with sl st into 3rd of ch 5. *skip next 2 dc, 1 dc into next dc, [2 dc, ch 3, 2 dc] into next ch 3 sp, **1 dc into next dc.

This appears to be a little trickier! Take a deep breath and break down instructions that are more challenging, like this one. One sewing and one guideline at a time, work them both.

Between the first and second single asterisks (*), you will crochet twice. in the preceding example. Proceed to the first single asterisk (*), then continue crocheting to the first double asterisk (**), and finally finish the step by joining with a slip stitch (sl st).

Using commas to separate steps is also beneficial. Reach the following comma, stop, and listen to the following directive. Anyone can become overwhelmed while trying to comprehend a line or two of abbreviated crochet words at first glance!

Using a Step-by-Step Crochet Pattern Reader

You succeeded, whoa! You gained knowledge of the fundamentals of crochet. The easy part is about to begin!

You'll note that almost every crochet design you use has a few standard components in addition to common crochet terminology. All the information you need to work up your project so that it works out perfectly is contained in these areas.

Prior to starting your project, it's critical to pay attention to the pattern information. You can avoid hours of headaches and aggravation by using the appropriate yarn and crochet hook size, measuring your gauge, and reading any critical pattern notes!

These are the typical sections found in the majority of written crochet patterns.

Pattern Title and Description

A title and a brief description will be the first elements of your pattern. A difficulty level is also included in or close to the description. Patterns can be categorized as easy, intermediate, advanced, or beginner.

Skill Level

Beginner: These patterns often work with a single color and incorporate simple shaping and stitches. These patterns may contain single, double, and treble crochet stitches as introductions. It's possible that you'll also see other acronyms like sl, st, and ch. Simple granny squares, washcloths, and crochet scarves are some examples of beginner patterns.

Easy: Easy designs are comparable to patterns for beginners, but they may require a little more skill to accomplish things like color changes and shaping. Crochet headbands and beanies are two examples of beginner-friendly patterns.

Intermediate: More shape, textures, and color shifts are typically present in these patterns. Creating interesting textures with a range of more intricate stitches, including as puff stitches and bobbles, is a common feature of intermediate patterns. Alternatively, your pattern can utilize easy stitches but more challenging yarn, such in a lace pattern or a pattern with a lot of fluffy yarn that makes counting stitches more challenging.

These patterns are intended for crocheters with extensive experience. Complex techniques, stitches, varied colorwork, and intricate shapes are used in advanced patterns. Expert crocheters can work on intricate afghans, clothes, and doilies, among other crafts.

Yarn, Tools, and Notions

The kind of yarn and materials you'll need to gather for your project will then be visible to you.

This is an illustration of the materials required to make a sunburst granny square.

H (5.0 mm) is the hook.

Yarn: Category 4 Worsted Weight Yarn

Additionally, you'll need:

- yarn needle; -

stitch markers, if preferred; -

tape measure or ruler

To make sure that your project turns out perfectly, gather a sufficient amount of the right kind of yarn and the right size hook. The final size, shape, and texture of your product might vary greatly depending on the hook size and yarn weight you use.

You may find out exactly how much yarn you need by using many patterns. The design might read, for instance, "1 skein (300 g/10.5 oz) of Bernat Blanket Yarn." Alternatively, it may indicate a specific amount of yarn or yardage, such as "220 yards (201 meters) or Bernat Blanket Yarn."

Sizes and Measurements

The majority of patterns will tell you what size your project should end up being. On a baby blanket pattern, for instance, this section would say, "Finished size: 30 x 34 inches."

Again, it's crucial to use the appropriate size yarn and hook and to check your gauge if you want to make sure your crochet creation finishes to the appropriate size.

Gauge

You'll notice a "gauge" portion in the directions if size matters for the pattern. Prior to starting your project, crochet a gauge swatch to make sure the finished product will be precisely the proper size. Imagine designing a lovely article of apparel only to have it not fit!

The recommended number of stitches and rows per 4-inch square will be specified in many patterns. The gauge for our simple crochet beanie design may be found here.

Gauge: 12 sts and 7.5 rows per 4".

This indicates that you should have 12 stitches and 7.5 rows in a 4-inch square.

Certain patterns specify gauge differently, particularly those that are worked in the round. An example of gauge instructions for a simple and entertaining bucket hat pattern can be found below.

"Crochet the Crown part of the hat pattern (Rounds 1–13) and measure the circle's width to determine your gauge. Its width should be 6.5 inches.

You should use a little larger hook if your circle is too tiny, which indicates that your crochet is too tight. You should use a little smaller hook if your circle is too big, which indicates that your crochet is too loose.

As mentioned, you might need to use a hook that is a little bit bigger or smaller if your gauge swatch doesn't turn out correctly.

Stitch Abbreviations and Terms

Are you feeling anxious about all of the crochet jargon and acronyms we discussed at the start of this article? Do not fret! Luckily, most patterns will indicate which abbreviations to expect. Usually, they'll also refresh your memory on the meanings of such abbreviations.

You will probably also notice instructions for any unusual or custom stitches that are utilized.

An illustration of the stitches used in the bucket hat pattern may be found here.

- ch stand for chain
- inc stand for increase
- sc stand for single crochet
- sc flo stand for only one crochet made through the front loop
- sl st stand for slip stitch
- st/sts: stitch/stitches

Most of the time, patterns that require crochet charts or diagrams will also be found in this section.

Pattern Notes

Usually, you can find any extra instructions for your specific design here in the pattern notes. These might consist of:

- Whether US or UK words are used in the pattern's writing.
- when working a pattern in rounds or rows.
- Which side is right and which is wrong?
- Whether a design is meant to be seamed or worked in one piece.
- Anything more the designer feels would be useful.

Main Pattern Instructions

Lastly, the primary pattern instructions are located here. Here's when knowing standard crochet terminology and stitch abbreviations come in handy.

To make sure you can understand a pattern on your own, let's have a look at an example of some pattern instructions.

We'll utilize the third round of this easy granny square. We'll convert the instructions into plain language beneath each step.

Round 3:

1. Chain 3 (one double crochet)

Chain 3 stitches. This appears to be the same as one double crochet when you come to the following row.

2. Next, work 2 dc, ch 1 into the ch-1 gap from the previous round, right below.

There was a chain stitch space in the previous round. Make two double crochets in that spot, and then chain one. You've got a granny cluster now.

3. Work three dc, ch 3, and three dc, ch 1 into the next ch-3 corner spot.

Three chain stitches form the space in the corner of the row that was previously crocheted. Work 3 double crochet, 3 chain stitches, 3 double crochets more, and 1 chain stitch in this place.

4. Work 3 dc and 1 ch-1 into the next ch-1 gap.

There will be another gap created with one chain stitch after that. Work 3 double crochets in this place, followed by 1 chain stitch.

Go back to the starting chain and repeat steps 3 and 4 there. Lastly, join at the top of the starting 5 ch-3 with a sl st.

Return and carry out steps 3 and 4 until you have completed the square. Use a slip stitch to join the yarn when you get back to the initial three chains you worked in step 1. You've completed a whole row on your granny square now!

Where can I acquire crochet designs the most easily?

You can follow a wide variety of crochet designs now that you understand the fundamentals of reading crochet instructions! Wonderful patterns may be found anywhere, with many of them being available for free.

To locate thousands of free patterns online, use a search engine.

Additionally, you may purchase designs online from websites like Etsy.

You can purchase books at your neighborhood craft store or online if you're seeking for a compilation of crochet patterns.

In conclusion, a lot of yarns will even have amusing designs inscribed on the tags. (This makes sure you're purchasing the right yarn for the pattern much easier!) Now that you know how to read a written pattern, there's no shortage of locations to locate enjoyable crochet projects.

BOOK 3:
CROCHET MISTAKES, TRICKS AND SECRETS

No matter how skilled the crocheter is, errors might still occur. The conundrum then becomes one of what to do: should one go back and correct the error or continue working with it? When the error occurs multiple rows ago, the issue is exacerbated.

According to an unofficial survey, the majority of people—knitters or crocheters alike—will go back and correct the error even if it has no bearing on the pattern. Reasons for fixing it ranged from the fact that I detest mistakes to the fact that no one else would notice it but I would know it exists. This makes sense in the situation of a dropped stitch. Nobody desires to witness the akin of a sprint in the midst of a complex shawl. Lacework makes sense as well.

However, nobody enjoys wasting time. That includes going back and correcting an error that has no effect on the pattern. Here are three suggestions for embracing errors made when crocheting or knitting.

Think of it as a signature. Painters and other traditional media artists are expected to sign their pieces. The only ways to design an item in fiber arts are by making a mistake or adding a tag.

Establish a deadline. Establishing a deadline for a project's completion can frequently make mistakes more acceptable. Sometimes it takes longer to go back and correct a small error than it does to finish the assignment. It's usually preferable to make the necessary corrections rather than ripping back to the mistake or frog it and start over if it doesn't affect the main pattern or can be easily fixed, such connecting two stitches together.

Treat the work with kindness. Rips and/or frogging can be tough on yarn, depending on its fiber composition and plies count. For example, loose or single plies are easily separated. If you want to be kind to the work, you should either gently undo the mistake or, if that is not possible, leave it alone.

Assemble it into the design. You can determine that an error is part of the design if it occurs early in the pattern or if you find yourself making the same error repeatedly. If you are neglecting important steps like increases or reductions for shape, this advice won't work; nevertheless, if you discover, for example, that you've been rotating your cables in the wrong way, you may just keep doing it regularly.

Although mistakes are unavoidable, the worry that comes with them isn't. These pointers can aid in reducing project stress.

CROCHET TROUBLESHOOTING TIPS

Here are some helpful crochet tips for beginners and crochet troubleshooting guidance if you're new to crocheting and are having issues!

It won't always be easy going when you're initially starting off with crocheting. Finding your rhythm and learning how to crochet properly while relaxing with your hook can take some time, which can result in certain crochet issues. Some of these crochet beginner hints and troubleshooting strategies will help you identify the areas where you're making mistakes if your crochet doesn't look quite right.

Why don't my crochet chains look right?

Everyone who wants to learn crochet should start by learning how to make chains. It takes some effort, so don't worry if yours don't seem absolutely neat the first time. Here are a few distinct factors that may be causing you problems with your chains.

My crochet chains are twisting around

Among the most frequent issues that novices get into when they try chains is probably this one. A chain of crocheted 'V' shapes should be arranged neatly on the same side, but occasionally your chain will appear twisted and the Vs will be on opposite sides. This typically happens as a result of shifting tension and either too-tight or too-loose chains—a topic we'll address next.

Sometimes, new crocheters have trouble knowing which way to wrap their yarn around their hook to form chains. If you make a mistake and swap directions, your chains may twist and kink. Since most crocheters twist their hook around the yarn instead of really wrapping the yarn around the hook, this can be difficult for some people to understand. Whenever you look at your hook from the base, the yarn should always be rotating counter-clockwise. An other way to look at it is that the yarn begins at the bottom, travels to the rear of the hook, crosses the top of the hook to the front, and then descends back to the bottom, where the hook is used to catch it.

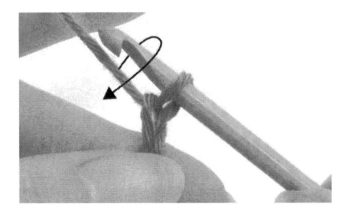

My crochet chains are too tight

A common mistake in crocheting is incorrect tension, so if you're having trouble making chain stitches, this could be the cause. Some crocheters have trouble because they are not relaxed enough, which leads to an excessively tight tension. See the chapter on how to hold a crochet hook if you're having trouble with this.

Your active loops will grasp too closely to the hook if your tension is too tight, as the example below illustrates. As a result, the loops will become extremely rigid and challenging to remove from the hook.

Pulling the following loop through this loop will be challenging for you because the resulting chains will be very tiny. Additionally, it will be challenging to get the hook into the chains when you begin working stitches into them.

If you're holding the hook with your right hand and your non-hook hand is your left, then try unwinding the working yarn from a few fingers on that hand to address the problem. As a result, there should be less strain on the yarn and you should be able to relax the active loops to sit farther away from the hook while still leaving a little gap, as demonstrated here.

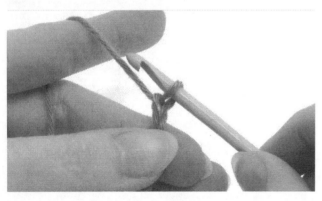

Another frequent issue that causes tight chains is holding your active loops at the hook's neck. You must ensure that the loops are made at the hook's wider shank in order to remedy this issue.

One of our favorite crochet tips is provided here if you're still having issues with a tight chain. Consider using a hook that is somewhat larger than the one you typically use for your yarn. For this course, for instance, we've been using a DK yarn and a 4mm hook. If you switch to a 5mm hook, you will see that larger chains can be produced even with very tight tension.

Try conducting a quick test if you're unsure if the chains you constructed are the proper size. Try putting your 4mm hook into the chains you've produced and let go of the larger 5mm hook. While each chain should be moderately snug around the hook, the hook should also fit into the chains rather easily.

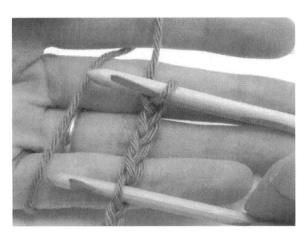

My crochet chains are too loose

A different issue that some novice crocheters encounter is slack tension. This is how you resolve that problem.

Your active loops will be too far away from the hook if your tension is too loose, as the example below illustrates. This will make controlling the loops on the hook challenging and...

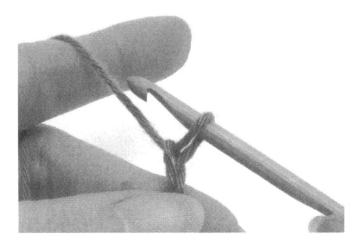

When you start sewing stitches into the large, resultant chains, they will appear unkempt.

Try wrapping the working yarn over additional fingers on your non-hook hand (your left hand if you're holding the hook in your right hand) to see if that helps fix the problem. By doing this, you should be able to tighten the active loops such that they sit close to the hook but leave a small space, as demonstrated here. This should also increase the tension on the yarn.

CROCHET TIPS FOR STRAIGHT EDGES

After you have improved your crochet chains, many novice crocheters encounter a problem: their edges are not straight. Two things usually cause this: stress and missed stitches! Your side edges and bottom width edge may be impacted by this. We'll investigate the possible causes of this so you can achieve the ideal look for your crochet! We'll be looking at crochet suggestions for straight edges using double crochet (dc) stitches in this first section.

Why does my first row of crochet stitches look wrong?

This is an illustration of a proper initial row of 10 dc stitches worked into 11 ch (keep in mind that dc stitches need an additional ch for the turning ch). Counting the tiny "v" shapes along the fabric's edge or the plaited chain-like shapes along the top will allow you to make sure.

The most frequent error that might occur when attempting the practice row mentioned above is forgetting to skip a chain. It's simple to complete, and since we missed a chain, we only have 9 DC. The only way to undo your work is to take off the hook and pull on the yarn until you get to the skipped chain. This demonstrates why it's critical to count your stitches at the end of every row; if the mistake is missed until the following row, there will be additional work to be done!

Working tight stitches is another typical problem. This will pucker the chain and result in the loops at the bottom looking saggy, as the example below illustrates. In addition to being shorter than they should be, tight stitches can also result in sizing issues. For instance, five regular rows may typically measure five centimeters, but five tight rows may only measure three. Try to release some of your tension by unwrapping the working yarn from a few fingers, and make sure the loops are made at the hook's shank rather than its neck in order to address this issue.

Achieving a tidy fabric in crochet requires maintaining a consistent tension, so master this technique from the start to avoid disappointment. Uneven stitches result from varying tension; as seen below, some are taller and more loosely spaced, while others are tighter. Don't worry if your first row looks like this—every rookie crocheter's first row looks like this! The secret to making things appear nicer is to practice hooking stitches until they become familiar, comfortable, and reliable.

My double crochet sides aren't straight; why is that?

Your side edges are another place where your crochet edges could appear incorrect. Again, this could be a case of missing stitches, so be careful to count your stitches as you did in the previous example. Uneven edges, however, can also result from misplaced or absent turning chains.

The general rule for double crochet rows is to start each row with one chain (ch1); Should you be working your first row into chains, you will begin your first stitch into the second chain, skipping the first chain. This is the turning chain, or t-ch, and it's essential to have straight and tidy rows. Using the t-ch allows you to raise the hook to the appropriate height needed for the height of stitches you plan to make. We only need to create one chain for double crochet since it is the smallest standard stitch; however, double crochet stitches do not count as stitches. Three chains would need to be made in order to reach the proper height for a taller stitch, such as treble crochet.

After creating the t-ch, continue working in dc stitches as usual. This is how your completed row of double crochet stitches should look: because of the t-ch, every double crochet is perfectly spaced at the same height from the first to the final stitch.

The initial dc is more tougher to work and the finished row will resemble this if you neglect to work the t-ch (it's easy to forget!). This is because the first dc is too low, creating a slope at the beginning of the row. While it may not seem like much at first, if you kept making the same mistake on every row, it would quickly become a significant issue.

My treble crochet sides aren't straight; why is that?

Many novices who are starting to treble crochet have trouble with their side edges at first. Your turning chain may be the cause of uneven side edges while working with treble crochet stitches, or any stitch taller than a double crochet. To determine the height of your treble stitches, create a turning chain of ch3 using the treble crochet stitch. This ch3 turning chain counts as your first stitch in treble crochet, thus you must take it into consideration while creating your first real treble stitch.

As such, when you make your first genuine treble stitch, you should treble crochet into the second stitch along, not the first stitch at the base of your turning chain. Because the turning chain counts as a stitch, if you create a treble crochet in the first stitch, you are actually producing an increase. If you complete this right, there will be a more noticeable gap and it will appear to be tilting slightly, but this will be fixed when you work the following row.

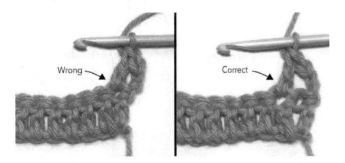

Upon finishing a row of treble crochet, it's possible to overlook your final stitch. You must work the last treble crochet stitch of the row into the top of the ch3 turning chain since it counts as a stitch. Every row that passes if you skip this step will result in fewer stitches. It will also help the turning chain stand up a little more evenly and lessen the noticeable gap when you put your final stitch into it.

My crochet curls; why is that?

You may notice that your first piece of crocheted cloth is curling and not resting flat, especially within the first row or two. Usually, as you work more rows, this will lessen, but it can also happen if the tension in your crochet is a little too tight, particularly with your crochet chains, as we discussed previously. However, some curling is normal, and even seasoned crocheters will occasionally suffer some natural curling. The primary method to address this is to block your crochet, which entails pinning out and moistening your crochet fabric; the act of wetting the yarn aids in relaxing the fibers.

How can I switch out the yarn?

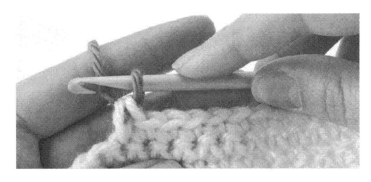

When crocheting, there are a few reasons you might want to switch up your yarn: perhaps you've run out of the current color, or maybe you just want to switch things up.

A few beginning crochet hints will come in handy when it comes to changing yarn. Initially, although it may seem appealing to simply tie a knot between the two strands and continue crocheting, it is preferable to do a thorough crochet join. This is because, in addition to the fact that you will be able to feel any knots on your final crochet fabric, a simple knot is more likely to come undone than a perfect crochet join when the cloth stretches and moves after you cut your yarn tails.

The same holds true if you discover a knot in the center of your ball of yarn—it happens, but it's irritating. Again, it may be tempting to just keep crocheting, but once you feel that unsightly knot in the midst of your stitches, you will wish you hadn't. Cutting off the knot and correctly re-knotting the yarn is always preferable. Additionally, there are a few methods for creating a seamless join between two pieces of yarn by employing the Russian or felted join techniques.

How Can I Change the Color in Crochet?

For the majority of beginner crochet projects, you can change colors using the basic crochet join technique described above. However, what if you wanted to use a lot of colors or alter them in a number of different contexts? This is the point at which learning crochet colorwork is beneficial. Fair Isle, Intarsia, and Tapestry crochet are the three basic methods used in crochet colorwork. The three ways share the same basic connecting procedure as previously described, but they offer distinct alternatives for handling the different yarns in between color changes. One of our favorite crochet techniques for novices is the tapestry crochet, which involves working your new stitches over the yarn you just changed from. This is a helpful technique to know when switching yarns because it helps to conceal your yarn end and seal your connection.

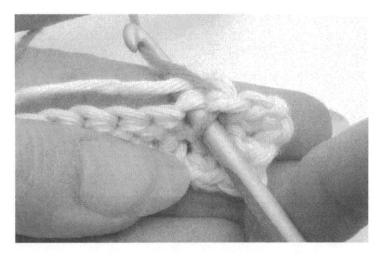

You'll need to learn how to weave in your crochet ends and fasten off crochet when your project comes to a conclusion. There are a few things to consider while looking for crochet tips for weaving in ends. The purpose of weaving in your ends is to prevent them from unraveling. Keep in mind that your crochet will likely be stretched and worked, so if you haven't done it correctly, the ends may work themselves loose. It is crucial to weave your ends through various sections of the stitches and back and forth several times. To attempt to secure your end, you may also try weaving over the same areas. Although it could be tempting to add a knot to make it extra secure, if you've woven in your ends well, your tying off should be the only knot you require. Stretching your crochet a little after you've determined your end is secure and you're okay with cutting your yarn near it might help the cut end slide into your work and vanish!

It's vital to keep in mind that everyone finds crocheting a little perplexing at first. We hope that these crochet ideas have helped you with your beginning crochet problems. Continue practicing and being persistent.

BOOK 4.
CROCHET PROJECTS FOR BEGINNERS.

A lifetime skill, crocheting is a delicate technique that you may use to create lovely gifts for others as well as items for your home and clothing. Beginner crocheters begin by learning a few foundational stitches, then progressing to more complex ones. Determine which style and size of hook is most comfortable for you first. After that, pick easy yarns and basic patterns, and you'll become an expert quickly.

Start by following these easy instructions in this crocheting how-to for beginners.

How to Crochet for Beginners

Choose a Crochet Hook and Yarn

All you need to start crocheting is a few basic ingredients. The crochet hook is the essential item, and it comes in a wide variety of sizes and styles. Aluminum is a great material for novice crochet hooks since it will allow the yarn to slide more smoothly.

The following three basic crocheting supplies are required:

• An aluminum crochet hook size I-9 or H-8, whichever feels best in your hand

• A skein or ball of wool or acrylic yarn
• Scissors

EASY CROCHET PATTERNS FOR BEGINNERS

POTHOLDER

You will enjoy to crochet these simple, double-thick crochet potholders repeatedly since they are quick and simple to complete. Making a crochet potholder is quick and easy with this free design, which uses a straightforward mix of fundamental crochet stitches. Additionally, the potholders are machine washable and long-lasting because they are composed of cotton yarn.

You'll adore this crochet potholder pattern whether you want to keep them all for yourself, sell them at craft fairs, or give hot pads as gifts.

How to Crochet a Potholder

You will learn how to crochet a square potholer that folds in on itself to provide the fabric double thickness by following this pattern. Chain stitch is used to begin, single crochet rounds follow, and a basic mattress or whip stitch is used to finish.

You will begin by crocheting a chain stitch. Down one side of the chain and up the other, crochet a single crochet.

Next, continue to single crochet in rounds around and around. To get a lovely texture, I like to knit the single crochet in the back loop. You will observe that the sides begin to expand, turn over, and become a potholder that is angled.

Then, to make a double-thick flat potholder, all you need to do is sew it together.

Double Thick Potholder Pattern

Skill Level: Easy

Materials

- Cotton yarn, 100 yards, worsted weight (category 4).
- Hook size H (5 mm) for crochet.
- Needle for yarn.
- Scissors.
- Tape Measurement.
- Insulated Lining Fabric is optional.

Size

Square potholder, 7 in. by 7 in. By creating a longer or shorter beginning chain, you can create a potholder that is larger or smaller.

Guage.

Ten rows x Fifteen sts = Four in.

Meeting gauge is not necessary unless you wish to create a potholder with a particular size.

if you wish to create thick, dense cloth by crocheting at a tight enough gauge. Size H hooks are ideal because they provide the proper gauge for a flexible hot pad that is dense enough to shield your hands from the heat. You will get a denser cloth with a smaller hook (G), but it will require more yarn. You'll use less yarn and get a more open cloth with a larger hook.

Stitch Abbreviations

The stitch abbreviations that are used in the pattern are listed below. Note: US words are used in the pattern.

CH: chain

SC: single crochet

SC BLO: only one back loop in a single crochet. Hook should be inserted into the stitch's back loop. Yarn over and pull through the final two loops on the hook.

SL ST: slip stitch

Instructions

Chain forty. (To begin with, use a chain that is 10 inches long for a 7-inch square.)

Round 1: SC two chains away from the hook. Don't work on the back hump; only work on the top loop. SC up until the beginning chain's end in each chain. In the last chain, make one extra SC.

Work your way around, sc once in each chain on the opposite side of the beginning chain. In the final chain, add one extra stitch. (Eighty stamens)

Start round one   End of round one

Round 2: SC BLO in each stitch around, starting at the top of the first stitch. (80)

Rounds 3 through 17: SC BLO in every stitch around, working in spiral rounds, which are continuous rounds. Stitch until the piece is half the height and half the width.

Work until the object is 5 inches tall, for instance, if your starting chain of 40 chain stitches measured 10 inches. That made a total of 17 rounds for me.

The potholder should be folded. A diagonal seam is produced by folding the top edges in toward the middle. Verify that the edges will meet when the piece is folded. It is likely that additional stitches will be required to ensure that your final stitch is in a corner.

Make a Hanging Loop.

If you want to hang the potholder from a hook, you may also create a loop. Chain 12 ch sts to achieve this. Next, sl st to the chain's beginning.

Sew the potholder together.

Cut yarn, leaving a 24 in. yarn tail, and pull through.

At the seam, match the stitches. Sew up the diagonal seam using either a whip stitch or a mattress stitch. I used a mattress stitch under one loop on each edge to create the image above.

Use a yarn needle to weave in the ends. If desired, block.

Pattern Variations

Here are several ways to personalize this pattern and make it uniquely yours.

Increase the amount of insulation. Before sewing the seam, place a square of Insul-Bright in between the layers of this potholder to increase its heat resistance.

Try using two cotton yarn strands held double in place of one yarn strand. You will need to use a larger hook size if you attempt this. Additionally, a shorter foundation chain could be a better place to start. Recall that you must begin with a 10-inch long starting chain in order to obtain a 7-inch finished square potholder.

Use HDC in place of SC. I think that using SCBLO for every round in the design above gives the potholder a fantastic texture with less diagonal lines. However, you may simply substitute another stitch, such as a half double crochet or another straightforward textured stitch, for the single crochet stitches. Remember that if you use a taller stitch, such as half double crochet, you might need to work in a few rounds of crochet.

Make the size bigger or smaller. You can simply build a longer or shorter beginning chain to change the potholder's size. Use an 8.5 in beginning chain for a 6 in. square potholder. Use an 11.5 in beginning chain for an 8 in square potholder.

Create a pillowcase. This pattern can even be enlarged to make a cushion cover. You would need to start with a 25-inch beginning chain if you wanted an 18-inch pillow. Next, stuff the pillow form in before finishing the seam.

EASY CROCHET SCARF PATTERN

With the help of this free crochet pattern, you can create an elegant and sophisticated ribbed scarf that appears complicated but is actually quite simple! It's a fantastic method for novices to pick up the fundamentals of crocheting without feeling overly complicated or discouraged.

It is simple to use even if you have never handled a hook before thanks to our step-by-step tutorial! To make it, all you need is some practice with basic crochet stitches; a thorough understanding of crochet patterns is not necessary.

Just two stitches are needed for this stylish, unisex scarf, which makes it an ideal project for novices: chain stitch and half double crochet (hdc). We will guide you through every step, starting with the basic chain stitches and ending with the fringe.

This free scarf design is ideal if you want to learn how to crochet or if you just need a quick project. The finest aspect? It takes only approximately two hours to complete from start to finish!

Scarf Pattern Variations

Here are some ways you might alter this pattern to make it more your own.

Size: Making longer or shorter scarves is simple with the adjustable pattern. Reduce the number of stitches in your starting chain to create a shorter scarf. Increase the number of stitches in your starting chain to create a longer scarf.

Fringe: The scarf's short ends can be adorned with fringe. You might need to use a third skein of yarn if you decide to add fringe.

Variation on the Infinity Scarf: You can sew the scarf's two short ends together to create an infinity scarf made of crochet. You can wear the scarf around your neck by double-up, large loop of cloth that is created when the scarf is sewn.

Materials

- Super bulky yarn.
- 9mm crochet hook, size N.
- Crochet needle (similar to a tapestry needle with a blunt point).
- Scissors.
- Tape Measurement.

Are you curious about the number of yarn skeins required for this crochet scarf pattern? Approximately two skeins will be required if you use Wool-Ease Thick and Quick. If you wish to add fringe to your scarf or make it longer, grab an extra skein.

Stitches and Abbreviations

- st/sts stands for stitch/stitches
- ch stands for chain
- hdc stands for half double crochet
- BLO stands for back loops only

Special Stitches

The majority of stitches will only be created in the back loops. This is referred to in the pattern as BLO.

What does "back loop only" mean?

A row of crochet stitches forms a small V-shaped pattern when you look at the top of the row. The section of the V that is closest to you is called the front loop, and the one that is furthest from you is called the rear loop. Hold a piece of crochet fabric with the Vs on top.

To start a new stitch, you would normally insert your hook beneath both the front and back loops. You will just place the hook beneath the back loops in the majority of the stitches in this design, skipping the front loops.

Pattern

The Terms used in this pattern is American.

Work the scarf in lengthwise rows, working flat back and forth.

There is no stitch count for the turning ch-2.

The beginning and last hdc stitches of each row should be worked beneath both loops to give you a smoother edge, even though practically all hdc stitches will be worked through the back loop.

Instructions

Tie a slip knot as the initial step. The slip knot is used to secure the yarn to the crochet hook.

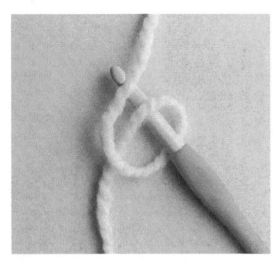

How a Slip Knot Is Tied

- Create a loop with the yarn, leaving a 6-inch tail.
- From front to back, pass the crochet hook into the middle of the loop.
- Grasp the yarn with the ball end and raise a loop.
- Pulling on both yarn ends will tighten the slip knot.

Crochet the Starting Chain

Making the initial chain is the next stage in crocheting a scarf. A starting chain, often referred to as a foundation chain, is a set of chain stitches in crochet that serves as the framework for the remainder of the scarf.

To make a chain stitch:

- Hook into the slip knot, draw up a loop by pulling the yarn over the hook.
- In order to create more chain stitches, repeat these steps.

If you have a propensity to chain too tightly, you may make the chain stitches with a 10mm or 12mm hook and then crochet the remaining scarves using a 9mm hook.

Make 126 chain stitches to begin this pattern.

Do not count the loop on your hook or the slip knot as stitches when calculating the number of chains you have produced.

Row 1

By crocheting into the beginning chain, you will create the first row. To start a chain, insert the crochet hook into the chain stitch from front to back. The hook's point will go through the V's center.

Alternatively, you can flip the chain over and begin the first row of stitches into the bumps on the back of the chain. You can choose to work into the back bar, which some people think gives a project a more polished edge.

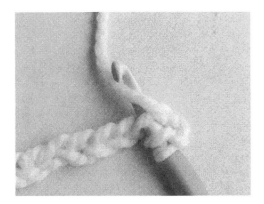

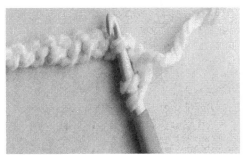

Row 1: Make 124 hdc beginning in the third chain from the hook. Turn (124 seconds)

Recall that the turning chain in this pattern does not count as a stitch.

Alternate Start: Rather than beginning with a lengthy chain, more seasoned crocheters could prefer to begin with foundation hdc stitches. Make 124 fhdc if you would rather begin with foundation stitches.

Row 2

In the first and last stitches of the second row, you will work a regular half double crochet; in the remaining stitches, you will work hdc-blo.

Row 2: Chain 2 (this is not a stitch). Begin with 1 hdc in the first stitch. Create 122 hdc blo. Make 1 hdc in the final stitch. (124 sts) Turn

Rows 3-10

Repeat Row 2 for the following few rows until the scarf is the desired width.

Rows 3-10: Chain 2 (this is not a stitch). Begin with 1 hdc in the first stitch. Create 122 hdc blo. Make 1 hdc in the final stitch. (124 sts) Turn

Finishing

Cut yarn and tie off when you have completed the last row. Weave in the ends after threading the yarn tails through a blunt-tipped tapestry needle or crochet needle.

Tips for Finishing your Scarf

Here are several methods for adding a polished finish to your scarf.

Enhance the Ends with Fringe

You can fringe your scarf all the way to the short ends if you'd like.

Cut forty 12-inch-long strands of yarn to create fringe. Each yarn strand should be folded in half to create a folded loop. Make sure the ends are equal by matching them.

From back to front, thread a crochet hook through a stitch. Grab two strands of yarn at the folded center point using the hook.

Partially pull the yarn pieces through the stitch.

Insert the yarn pieces' ends through the loops that have been folded.

To make the fringe more tightly, tug on the yarn ends.

Variation of the Infinity Scarf

To create an infinity scarf with crochet, sew the scarf's two short ends together to form a loop. The scarf's short ends should be matched, then sewn together using a mattress stitch.

Add the ends by weaving them in.

CHUNKY RIBBED BEANIE

With this simple Ribbed Beanie design, even beginners may learn how to crochet a hat. The simple stitch pattern used to create this crochet beanie is reminiscent of knit ribbing and is easy to recall. The end product is an elastic, textured fabric that knits and crochets like a dream! Crafted with a single skein of bulky-weight yarn, this project is suitable for both novice and experienced crocheters.

This simple crochet hat pattern is perfect if you're new to crocheting or just need something quick to work on while you watch Netflix.

Crochet Ribbing Stitch

Ribbing stitch worked in half double crochet is used to create the hat's body. The only result of working the hdc through the back loop is a stretchy crochet ribbing that works well for hats.

A few single crochet stitches are added to the hat's crown to provide the appearance of natural tapering. When it comes time to finish the hat and gather the opening, this will be helpful.

Pattern Variations

Sizes: Adult, teen, child, and toddler head sizes can all be easily accommodated by adjusting the design. We'll provide you with a hat sizing chart and an easy formula to use to ensure a great fit every time.

Brim: Its 12" height was intended to be long enough to fold over a beautiful, broad brim. We will show you how to modify the pattern if you would prefer your hat to not have a fold-over brim.

Style: This beanie has a more traditional beanie form rather than being overly baggy.

Pattern

Finished Size: Newborn through Adult

For the purposes of this pattern, we will be making an Adult Medium, or a hat length of 12" and a circumference of 20".

Gauge: 12 sts and 7.5 rows per 4". Check your gauge, and factor this into your size calculation.

Materials

- Yarn
- Hook
- yarn needle
- If desired, use stitch markers.
- If desired, use a ruler or tape measure.

Stitches & Abbreviations

- st/sts stand for stitch/stitches
- ch stand for chain
- sc stand for single crochet
- hdc stand for half double crochet
- BLO stand for back loops only

Unique Stitches

This is not a design for any unique stitches. However, you should be aware that practically all stitches will be produced just in the back loops. This is referred to in the pattern as BLO.

Notes

The terminology used in this pattern is American.

The hat is crocheted in rows, flat and back and forth.

The completed flat piece is then seamed to form a tube.

Subsequently, one end is collected to form the shape of the hat.

Pattern Instructions

This is a beginner-friendly crochet pattern for a winter hat.

We started by taking our measurements. Our desired hat has a brim and is 12 inches in length and 20 inches in circumference.

Row 1: Chain 36, then 30 hdc in the second chain from the hook. 5 sc. (35 stitches)

Row 2: Chain 1, 5 sc blo, 30 hdc blo starting in the same (first) stitch. (35 stitches)

Row 3: Chain 1, 30 hdc blo, 4 sc blo, 1 sc in the same (initial) stitch. (35 stitches)

Continue working in rows 2 and 3 until the crochet piece measures 20" along the long edge, or the size of the finished hat you had previously determined.

We worked 36 rows of crocheting for this hat.

Please take note that you should measure along the long edge of the half-double crochet stitches rather than the single crochet stitches. Since a fabric measuring tape is more flexible than a ruler in this situation, it is helpful.

Finishing: Seam the sides.

You're almost done, hooray! There are two seaming techniques to choose from when it comes time to sew the hat together.

1: The first alternative is to use a straightforward slip stitch seam to join the hat's sides. Work a final row of slip stitches through loops on both edges to create a slip stitch seam.

To carry out this: First, with the working row in front, fold the crocheted rectangle in half, right sides out. Make one more row of slip stitches, but this time, put your hook through the loops of the starting chain and the working row's back loop.

91

2: Alternatively, if you'd rather, you might use a mattress stitch seam to join the sides.

- With the right sides facing outward, align the beanie's two sides.
- A yarn tail that is roughly three times the length of the seam should be threaded through a yarn needle.
- After the first stitch on one side, insert the needle under the first stitch on the opposite side.
- Stitch the seam again, going back and forth. Make an effort to evenly space the stitches.
- Pull the yarn every few stitches to seal the seam. Don't overtighten; instead, aim to maintain a constant tension.
- Weave in the ends of the yarn once you have reached the seam's end.

Gather the top of the hat.

After putting the yarn through the final loop, cut the lengthy tail. Make long running stitches along the top edge of the hat with a darning needle and the yarn tail.

Gather the top edge of the hat by pulling the yarn tail, then fasten it shut. To secure the yarn tail, you can tie it. Add the ends by weaving them in.

CROCHET HAIR SCRUNCHIE

Have you ever considered making your own hair accessories out of crochet? Try this simple DIY hair scrunchie pattern to add a little handcrafted flair to your outfit.

Additionally, it's the ideal crochet pattern for novices. With only one easy stitch, these crochet scrunchies come together quickly. These scrunchies are easy to create if you know how to half double crochet.

How to Make Crochet Scrunchies

Depending on the type or appearance of the scrunchie you want to construct, there are a ton of various ways to crochet one.

Since we really wanted a big, fluffy, plush scrunchie for this pattern, we decided to crochet an elastic hair tie in the round.

This gives you loads of volume and ruffles by creating a crocheted tube around the hair tie.

Chain ten, then use a slip stitch to join to begin the scrunchie. Alternatively, you can construct ten FHDC if you know how to do foundation half double crochet.

Next, create a tube of fabric by crocheting half double crochet stitches around the hair tie in a spiral design.

There you have it. You may wear this adorable, thick scrunchie in your hair or on your wrist.

You can simply whip up a batch of these scrunchies to give to family and friends because they are so enjoyable to make. Even at the last minute, they make a wonderful homemade gift.

Additionally, these scrunchies are a fantastic product to produce and offer at flea markets and craft fairs. They are an easy-to-make, in-vogue item that requires little time to produce.

Easy Crochet Hair Scrunchie

A simple crochet pattern for hair scrunchies that can be produced for handcrafted presents or sold at craft fairs.

Use worsted yarn to make it as shown, or switch to velvet yarn for an interesting and delightful texture.

Materials:

worsted weight yarn

Tools:

crochet hook, size J

blunt tapestry needle

Instructions

Chain 10 using worsted weight yarn and a J crochet hook. Wrap the chain around a hair tie, being careful not to twist, and secure with a slip stitch to create the start of a tube.

Work 36 half double crochet rows, working in spiral rows. (Depending on the size of your hair tie, make more or fewer rows.)

Trim yarn, ensuring a long tail is left. Sew the tube's two ends together using the yarn tail and a blunt tapestry needle. Add the ends by weaving them in.

Notes

You may instead start with 10 FHDC instead of the 10 chain stitches if you choose.

CROCHET A GRANNY SQUARE

Would you like to know how to make a granny square in crochet? Granny squares are surprisingly simple to build, despite their very complicated appearance!

This guide will walk you through my simple granny square pattern, which is ideal for the self-assured beginner and easy to learn and memorize. Detailed directions and plenty of photographs are provided so you can learn how to crochet a traditional granny square.

You may create a granny square blanket, sweater, purse, or anything else you choose to make once you have mastered the fundamental granny square technique!

A granny square: what is it?

A traditional crochet motif is a granny square. Basic crochet stitches like the chain and double crochet are used to create it. A granny square's square form and lace-like appearance make it simple to identify.

Granny squares are a fantastic method to use up small scraps of leftover yarn because they are often small in size. You can use a different color of yarn for each round, or you can crochet granny squares in a single solid color.

Granny Square Variations

There are literally hundreds of ways to make granny squares. Granny hexagons as well as traditional granny squares, sunburst granny squares, solid granny squares, and solid granny squares without gaps can all be made!

However, we'll walk you through the traditional version in this article, which is composed of four rounds of double crochet clusters worked into chain gaps.

Granny squares made with this pattern lay flat, which is why we enjoy it. To keep them square rather than rounded, we utilize chain-3 gaps at the corners.

Supplies

A small quantity of yarn and the suitable size crochet hook are required to produce a granny square.

- Yarn
- Crochet hook
- A few stitching marks to mark the beginning of each round.

For this craft, any sort of yarn will work; a small amount from your stash would work just fine. Having said that, we always advise novices to choose with a smooth-textured, light-colored worsted weight yarn. (That way, it will be simpler to see your stitches.) Next, select a hook size according on the yarn label.

This basic granny square will be crocheted in a plain color. For each circle, you can either repeat the process or switch up the color of yarn.

Notes

The terms used in this crochet pattern are US terms.

Joined rounds are worked "in the round" to create the granny square.

For each cycle of this project, the right side is faced.

You will be working into the chain gaps from the previous round instead of the stitches from the previous round.

Stitch Abbreviations:

The basic crochet stitches are used to create the granny square. The acronyms used in this design are listed below.

- ch stands for chain stitch

- ch-sp stands for chain space
- dc stands for double crochet
- sl st stands for slip stitch
- st(s) stands for stitch(es)

Special Stitches

Chain spaces divide granny clusters, which form the rounds of the granny square.

Three-dc cluster, or granny cluster: Three double crochet stitches combined into one stitch or space is known as a granny cluster. Chain stitches are used in this pattern to keep the granny clusters apart from one another.

Three Ways to Begin a Granny Square

There are three methods for beginning a granny square. You can begin using the magic ring technique, a center ring of chain stitches, or a single chain stitch.

1: Begin with a single chain.

Fitting all of the stitches into a single chain stitch can be challenging, despite the technique's simplicity and speed.

Chain 3 to begin with a single chain stitch, then work the subsequent stitches into the initial chain stitch. The first chain stitch will be created from each of the clusters in the first round.

2: Center Ring Chain Stitch

Although this method is quick and simple, the hole in the center of your square will be more noticeable.

Starting with a center ring made with chain stitch: After chaining four stitches, combine your chain into a circle using a slip stitch. After that, work your first circle inside the circle.

3: Magic Circle, also known as Magic Ring

The magic ring, sometimes referred to as the magic circle technique, is the third choice. You'll get a tight center with no gaps or holes with this procedure.

Pattern

Center Ring:

Begin the granny square with a center ring.

Chain four times and insert your hook into the first chain stitch.

Then, combine the chain stitches into a circle using a slip stitch.

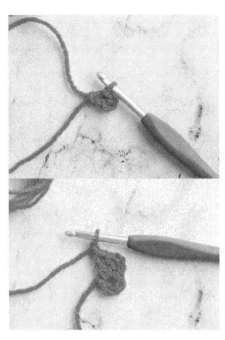

Round 1's initial cluster is crocheted.

Round 1

Chain (ch) 3. This counts as the granny cluster's initial double crochet (dc) stitch.

Work 2 dc into the center ring. Now, what appears to be three DC should be adjacent to each other. The first granny cluster is this one. Ch 3.

Proceed to create the second granny cluster now. Work 3 dc into the central ring. Ch 3.

Create the third cluster: Work 3 dc into the central ring. Ch 3.

Create the fourth cluster. Work 3 dc into the central ring. Ch 3.

At this stage, there should be four granny clusters, with the final ch-3 space at the end and ch-3 gaps between them at the corners. Slip stitch (sl st) is used to join the circle and form the square. The first round is now finished.

And here are the same Round 1 instructions again, in case you prefer the standard shortened version:

Round 1: Make 2 dc, ch 3, (3 dc, ch 3) three times into the central ring. Sl st to the top of the first ch-3.

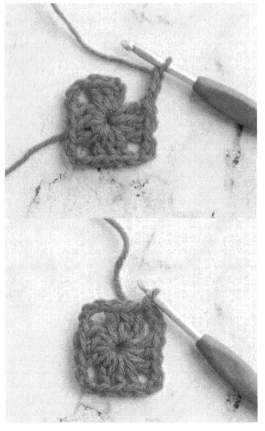

Round 1 is completed with a slip stitch join.

Round 2:

Chain 4. (This is the first dc and the first ch-1 gap.)

In the next ch-3 space (also known as the first corner space), work 3 dc, ch 3, 3 dc, ch 1.

For a total of three times, repeat Step 2 twice more.

Work: 3 dc, 3 ch, 2 dc in the final ch-3 space.

Sew in a slip stitch to the third chain from the start of the chain stitches.

That brings the second round to an end.

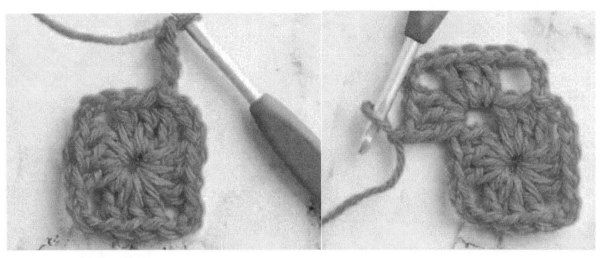

Making Round 2.

Round 3:

Chain 3. (This counts as 1 dc.)

Next, work 2 dc, ch 1 into the ch-1 space from the previous round, just below. (This completes this round's first granny cluster.)

Work three dc, ch 3, and three dc, ch 1 into the next ch-3 corner space.

Work 3 dc and 1 ch-1 into the following ch-1 space.

Go back to the starting chain and repeat steps 3 and 4 there. Lastly, join at the top of the beginning ch-3 with a sl st.

Crocheting Round 3.

Chain Round 4:

(This is 1 dc plus the ch-1 gap.)

Work 3 dc, ch-1 into the next ch-1 slot.

Work 3 dc, ch 3, 3 dc, ch 1 into the next ch-3 corner space.

Steps 2 and 3 should be repeated in each of the remaining ch-1 and ch-3 places.

Work 2 dc in the final ch-1 space.

Join at the top of the first ch-3 with a sl st.

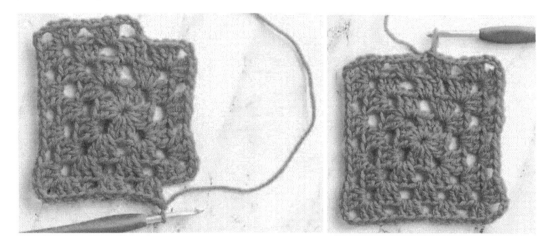

This completes Round 4.

How to Make Greater Granny Squares

To make the granny square as large as you like, add more rounds. Repeat rounds 3 and 4 until you get the desired size to make larger squares.

completing the Granny Square

After finishing the last round, cut your working yarn, leaving a tail that is six inches long. Insert the yarn into the final stitch. Tie in any loose ends with a blunt yarn needle.

There you have it! You've just completed a traditional granny square in crochet!

Granny Squares with Changing Colors

You can experiment with multi-colored granny squares once you've mastered the art of creating single-color ones.

Make a slip stitch join with the new color yarn at the end of the round to switch to a new color. (Recall that a slip stitch is used to join each round to the top of the starting ch-3.)

Book 5.
Crochet projects for intermediates

Lace Jewels Hooded Scarf Free Crochet Pattern

This hooded scarf made of crochet is a wonderful gift idea. The soft self-striping yarn creates amazing rows that highlight the open crochet lace.

The stitch pattern works up quickly once it is mastered. This is a fantastic application of the Lion Brand "Shawl in a Ball" and "Shawl in a Cake," which many of you may have noticed from Lion Brand's recent strong sales.

Size: 9" x 83"

Materials:

- "Shawl in a Cake" by Lion Brand, size 4 worsted weight yarn, 481 yards per 150g, 2 cakes of colorway Crown Jewels, about 700 yards utilized
- H-5 [5mm] hook is recommended.
- Tassel (optional) made with a yarn needle

Gauge

In stitch pattern, 28 stitches for 8 rows equals 4".

Special Stitches

In the appropriate stitch, work [dc, ch 3, dc].

Fan: dc in specified space, *ch 3, dc in same space, rep from * one more.

Crochet Pattern Instructions

Row 1: Work 66 sk 6 sc in next ch, dc in next ch, *sk 3 sc in next ch, sk 3 dc in next ch, [ch 3, dc in next ch] thrice, rep from * to last 9 scs, sk 3 sc in next ch, sk 3 dc in next ch, ch 3, dc in final ch, turn.

Row 2: *V-stitch (see Special Stitches above) in next sc, ch 5, rep from * to last sc, v-stitch in last sc, ch 2, sc in sp of start ch-6, turn.

When working the hdc in the stitch below, the chain-5 gap is likewise wrapped. It brings them together within the HDC.

Row 3 (RS): Ch 1, sc in first sc, *fan in ch-3 sp, hdc in fan's center dc below ch-5 sp, fan in last ch-3 sp, sc in last sc, turn. Rep from * to final ch-3 sp.

Turn. Row 4: Ch 4, dc in same sc, *ch 5, v-stitch in next hdc, rep from * to final sc, ch 5, [dc, ch 1, dc] in last sc, round.

Ch 6, dc in ch-1 sp, *hdc in center dc of fan below ch-5 sp, fan in next ch-3 sp, rep from * to final ch-5 sp, hdc in center dc of fan below, [dc, ch 3, dc] in sp of start ch-4, turn.

In row six, work as follows: Ch 1, sc in first dc, Ch 2, *v-stitch in next hdc, Ch 5, rep from * to last hdc, V-stitch in last hdc, Ch 2, sc in sp of start ch-6, turn.

Rows 7–170: Repeat rows 3-6 one after the other.

Row 171: Repeat row 3 and secure.

Seaming

Scarf should be folded in half. Sew along the line that measures 10" from the fold down

Tassel (optional)

Wind yarn around until you have a nice amount of strands using any sturdy object measuring about 9 inches.

Remove with care so that you can wrap a separate 10-inch length of yarn around the top and tie it off firmly. This is the tie that you will use to secure the hood's top. At the bottom, cut off every strand of the "ring." A further 10" of yarn should be attached approximately 1" below the top of the tassel.

Draw the ends of that strand inside the tassel with a yarn needle. Securely weave the ends of the tassel into the top of the hood.

Securely weave in ends using a yarn needle.

FLUFFY MERINGUE SHAWL

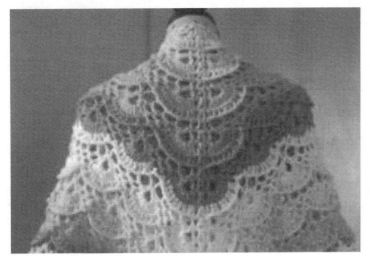

The Fluffy Meringue Shawl is an adaptation for the Yarnspirations Baby Blanket called the Fluffy Meringue Baby Blanket.

MOUNTAIN BREEZE PONCHO

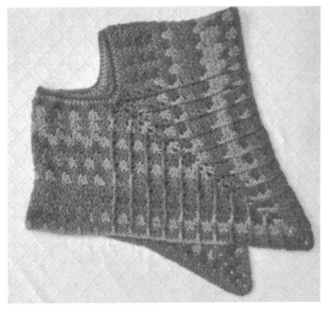

Wear this lovely Crochet Mountain Breeze Poncho with a nice top and jeans for a stylish yet functional look. The Mountain Breeze Poncho, created by Lorene Eppolite, is simple to put together with Red Heart Dreamy Stripes; the colors complement each other so well.

MOROCCAN TILE AFGHAN

Presenting the Afghan made of Crochet Moroccan Tiles. Rich coloring is possible with this afghan made with Bernat Velvet yarn. comparable to a Moroccan tile floor.

These oval-shaped motifs can be pieced together to create a lovely rectangular afghan with matching quarter and half motifs.

MOSAIC MOTIFS BLANKET

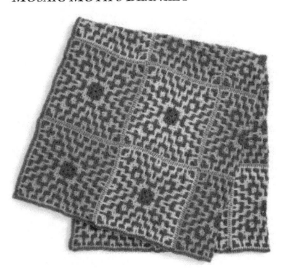

The Caron Mosaic Mosaic Motifs Blanket is this one.

It turns out that mosaics can be created with motifs, as I had wondered. It's quite the pattern! This one needs to be filmed—no, not for you, but for me! Here, let's set some clear priorities! hehe I have to learn it if I record it, so is that really so horrible?

BOOK 6.
CROCHET PROJECTS FOR ADVANCED

CROCHET PEPPERMINT THROW

There are amazing spirals in this festive afghan. This might be the year's best afghan, in my opinion. Give this fresh design a try.

SPIDERWEB BLANKET

I present the Jo-Ann Fabrics and Crafts Spiderweb Blanket, a fun and kid-friendly blanket.

This 12-point ripple afghan is colored to resemble a web of spiders. with a subsequent overlay added to produce the lines that shoot out from the middle.

This 55-inch-diameter afghan features three blue and three red sections, with white circles separating each section to give the appearance of a web. Finally, add the final details. The new Bernat Blanket Brights Yarn is being used for this. It is incredibly soft and colorful. These would be thoughtful presents for a loved one.

TEXTURED BAVARIAN PILLOW

Try this 12" pillow.

Huge, bulky pillows are trendy right now, but I prefer a mix of small and large pillows. This fulfills my desire for an evening project to be successful right away. You can quickly make a set of these. They don't take long to make.

These remind me of pillows given as wedding gifts.

BEAN STITCH BAG

Presenting Mikey's design, the Crochet Bean Stitch Bag. The bean stitch was created by Jeanne, and it's also quite addictive!

When using variegated yarn, this stitch can have a stunning appearance. The stitch creates appearances of texture that are thicker. It looks like the stitches are woven together. It provides additional strength to bags.

Additionally, the stitch prevents the variegation from repeating itself, which can occur when using the same stitch all the way through.

To create the bands of bead stitches seen in the sample, rows 2 through 9 must be repeated. View the tutorial's introduction to get a true idea of how it looks.

SCAN ME

SUN BLOSSOM MANDALA DOILY

The original Sun Blossom Mandala Doily by Diane Lavos for Red Heart was adapted into the Crochet Sun Blossom Alternative Mandala Doily.

Although I didn't mean to make a duplicate, any crocheter may encounter obstacles. Rather than giving up and destroying your work, you can imagine new possibilities for your circumstances.

BOOK 7.
AMIGURUMI CROCHET PROJECTS PATTERNS

Consider giving amigurumi a try. This collection of free amigurumi patterns features designs for dolls, food, animals, and more, suitable for crocheters of all experience levels.

Amigurumi: What Is It?

The Japanese word for stuffed toys made by crocheting or knitting is amigurumi. The most popular kind of amigurumi are crocheted ones, and they usually start with the single crochet, one of the most basic stitches. Even with the increases and reductions, color changes, and a few unique techniques, these are still enjoyable and simple crocheted items.

You can make them quickly because most of them are small and don't require a lot of yarn. You may play with them, display them on a shelf, hang them from a Christmas tree, or even use them as a keychain!

A RAINBOW OF MONSTERS

You'll need the following stuff:

- Small amount of worsted weight yarn
- Size E Crochet hook (or your favorite)
- Plastic safety eyes (we used 6 mm, but you can use whatever makes your monster happy!)
- Polyester fiberfill stuffing

- Embroidery floss
- White felt
- Craft glue
- Scissors
- Yarn needle
- Embroidery needle

Head/Body:

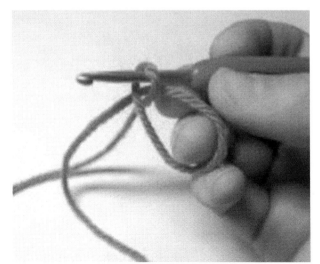

Start by using your yarn to create the illustrated ring.

Hook your working yarn (the yarn that comes from the ball) with the hook after inserting it into the front of the ring. Entwine a loop with your ring.

Pull the working yarn through the loop on your hook after encircling it from behind. This is written in the pattern "ch 1" and is referred to as a chain stitch.

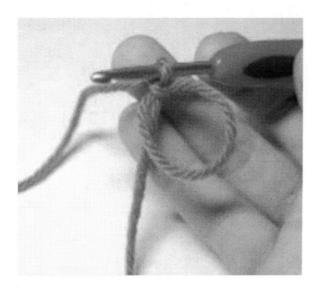

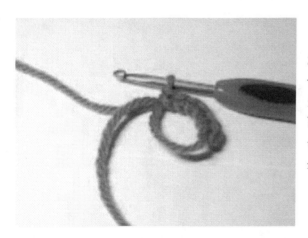

Six stitches will now be single crocheted into the ring. Pull up a working yarn loop to the front by inserting the hook into the front of the ring. You have two loops on your hook. Pull through both loops after encircling the hook with the working yarn from the back. In the ring, this is a single crochet stitch. Finish the ring with five more single crochets.

The stitches will gather together to form a circle as you seal the ring by pulling the short yarn tail. The foundation of the remainder of your monster is this.

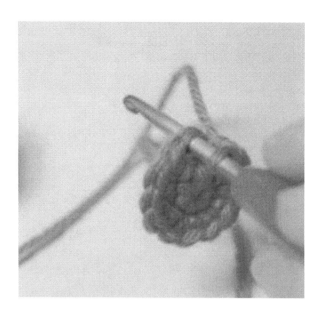

You will increase by crocheting twice into each stitch in order to expand the circle. As indicated, place your hook beneath both loops of the subsequent stitch.

Pull up a loop. Two loops are on your hook.

Encircle the hook with the working yarn. Stroke through both of the loops. This is a single stitch in crochet. Once more, single crochet into the same area. There has been an increase. In this round, you will repeat the instruction "2 sc into next st" for each stitch until you have 12 total stitches in the circle. Each "v" that is made around the circle counts the number of stitches.

You will increase in every other stitch in the following round. This indicates that you will work one stitch in the next stitch, two stitches in the next, and so on. 18 stitches should be on your needles at the end of the round.

or the final set of increases, you will go up a stitch every third. This implies that you will single crochet twice in the first stitch, once in each of the next two stitches, twice in the next stitch, and so on, until you have worked 24 stitches in all.

You should have a flat circle with 24 stitches around it once you have finished increasing. As you single crochet into each stitch for nine rows, this circle transforms miraculously into a cylindrical shape.

Once you have nine rows, continue crocheting around 24 stitches with a stitch marker, moving the marker to the loop on your hook and then crocheting around 24 more times. Of course, you can do more than nine rows to make your monster taller, or fewer than nine rows to make him rather small.

Complete the body of your monster by slip stitching into the subsequent stitch. To do this, just cut the yarn leaving a few inches on each end, slip your hook into the next stitch, pull up a loop, and pull that loop through the loop on your hook fully.

Base:

Repeat the first few steps to create a circle of 24 stitches, which will become the base of the monster.

Attach the eye(s) before you sew the components of your newborn monster together. Slice off the felt portion as needed. Two little circles, one big circle, etc. Make a small incision and place the safety eye's post in the desired location for the black eye. After positioning the eye on the body piece as desired, push the post through.

Position the washer over the post after inserting it into the body. Firmly press and fully lock the washer onto the post.

Stuff your monster with a modest amount of stuffing. Place the bottom piece over the body's bottom. Stitch the pieces together by aligning the stitches and sewing in between them using the long yarn tail and a yarn needle. Fill the hole to the required level as it closes.

Now is the time to create the expression for your monster. Using the embroidery needle and floss, add facial features to your monster, such as a mouth, eyebrows, and eyelashes.

Adhere a small felt piece to his mouth to give him one or two teeth. Imagination is key! To ensure that he looks perfect, you might first draw up your concept.

The edges of your monster's eyes should be sewn or glued down.

To add a bow, tie a strand of yarn into a bow and use the same color stitch to sew it onto your monster's head.

AMIGURUMI DUCK

I used:

Plush yarn Himalaya Dolphin Baby

Hook 5 mm

Safety eyes 9 mm

Toy filling

AMIGURUMI WHALE PATTERN

Join me as I go step by step in creating your very own amigurumi whale! His large domed head and flat belly make him the ideal shelf sitter!

AMIGURUMI TURTLE

It's easy enough for novices (I cover all the stitches and skills, too!). And simple and quick enough for experienced crocheters to finish in about an hour!

CONCLUSION

The best thing to do now that you've learned the fundamentals of crocheting is to get a hook and some yarn and practice, practice, practice! It's true that some individuals find crocheting really difficult at first, but persevere! After you've done them a few times, they'll start to get easier and make more sense, though the first few stitches may feel weird and seem a little off.

WHY YOU MUST ACQUIRE THIS SKILL

A few reasons to crochet frequently are listed below. Crocheting is a hobby that individuals of all ages can enjoy, not just grandmas.

Stress and anxiety can be lessened by crocheting.

Crochet is a fantastic alternative if you're seeking for a way to unwind and reduce tension. If you're a novice who is still learning how to crochet, you'll quickly discover that it's a great way to unwind and that it's not hard to learn with the correct online course.

A much-needed escape from the stress of daily life can be found in the repetitive motions of crochet.

Research has also demonstrated that crocheting can lessen the symptoms of anxiety and despair. According to one study, people who crocheted felt less stressed and more at ease than people who didn't.

You can get better sleep by crocheting.

You can enhance the quality of your sleep by crocheting. Crochet before bed can help you fall asleep more quickly and stay asleep longer if you have sleep problems. Crochet has calming qualities that can also aid in calming any racing thoughts or anxieties that are keeping you awake at night.

Crochet may be worth a try if you're looking for a way to get a better night's sleep. After a demanding day, crocheting can be a wonderful way to decompress and unwind.

You can feel happier by learning to crochet.

It has also been demonstrated that crocheting improves mood. According to a different study, people who crocheted felt more upbeat and joyful than people who didn't. Additionally, crocheting can aid in lowering tension and anxiety, which can improve mood.

Attempting to uplift your spirits by crocheting could be a worthwhile endeavor.

Opportunities to socialize are provided by crochet.

Taking up crocheting is also a terrific opportunity to meet new people and engage in social interaction. You can join a variety of online and offline crocheting organizations and groups, as well as crochet alongside friends and family. Whether crocheting at coffee shops or waiting areas, striking up a conversation with strangers is commonplace.

Moreover, crocheting can be a fantastic opportunity to meet new people and establish connections with like-minded individuals.

Creativity can be enhanced through crocheting.

Your creativity can also be enhanced by crocheting. Maya Angelou once said, "You can't use up creativity." You have more the more you use.

You'll be able to crochet increasingly elaborate and sophisticated designs as your skills advance. Crochet is a fantastic hobby if you're seeking for something to help you express yourself more creatively.

It's rewarding to crochet.

Making anything from scratch, even plush animals or soft blankets, can be a really creative and fulfilling endeavor. It feels fantastic to be able to turn a ball of yarn, a crochet hook, and a pattern into something useful! Making things for your home and yourself, as well as gifts for loved ones, is a fulfilling hobby.

You can maintain mental acuity by crocheting.

Additionally, crocheting helps maintain mental acuity since it demands focus and attention to detail, both of which can enhance focus and concentration. Additionally, crocheting helps maintain mental acuity and stave off cognitive deterioration as you age. Crochet is an excellent activity if you're seeking for something to keep your mind active.

Once you've learned the foundational stitches, everything else will start to make much more sense, and even the most difficult patterns won't seem so overwhelming. After that, you can advance to intermediate and beyond.

Happy crocheting.

Dear Crochet Enthusiast,

As we tie off the final stitch of our crochet journey together, I want to take a moment to express my deepest gratitude for allowing me to be a part of your crafting world. Your support has been the vibrant yarn that has woven this book into existence, and it's been an absolute joy to share my passion for crochet with you.

But our creative dialogue doesn't have to end here. In fact, it can blossom even further with your help. If you've found joy, inspiration, or even a new stitch or two within these pages, I kindly invite you to share your experience on Amazon.

Your feedback is incredibly important—not just to me, but to fellow crochet lovers and curious beginners who are considering joining our vibrant community. By leaving a review, you're not only guiding potential readers in their decision-making but also helping me understand what resonated with you, what you loved, and even what you'd like to see more of in the future. It's through your insights that I can continue to create content that uplifts, educates, and inspires.

Leaving a review is easy:

1. Head over to the Amazon website and log in to your account.

2. Find the book's page (a quick search for the title should bring it up).

3. Scroll down to the 'Customer Reviews' section and click on the 'Write a customer review' button.

4. Share your thoughts, experiences, and any favorite moments or projects from the book.

Whether it's a few words or a detailed account, every review is invaluable and greatly appreciated. Your voice has the power to inspire others and bring our wonderful community of crafters closer together.

Thank you for your support, your passion, and your willingness to share your journey. Together, we're not just crocheting; we're creating a tapestry of shared stories, experiences, and endless creativity.

Warmly,

Lana Dillard

Author & Fellow Crochet Enthusiast

Review this Book

To review the book frame the QR code

BONUS

Frame the QR code to download
your three special bonuses!

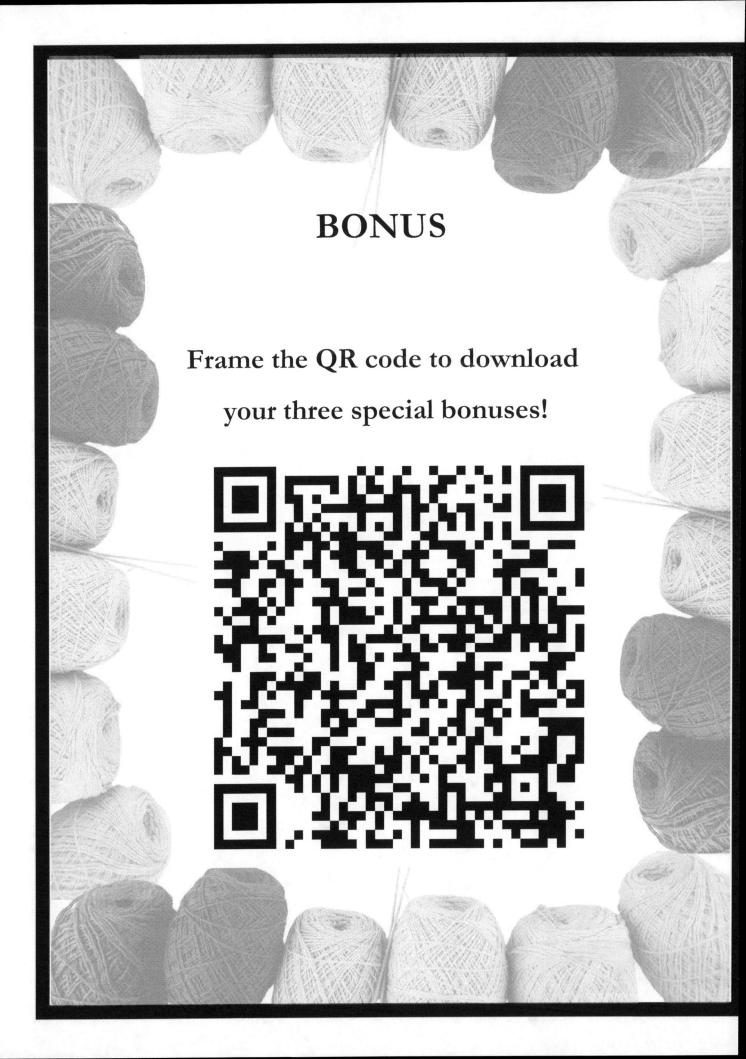

SUPER BONUS

Download this guide to make your own little

friends Step by Step

Made in the USA
Columbia, SC
08 September 2024

41776122R00070